Productivity is Power II

PRODUCTIVITY IS POWER II

For Creative, Business, and Other Professionals

HILLARY RETTIG

Infinite Art Press

Copyright © 2023 Hillary Rettig. All rights reserved.

Published in Kalamazoo, MI, USA.

Cover by Lee Busch/LBDesign, www.lbdesign.com
Formatting and interior design by Woven Red Author Services, www.wovenred.ca

Productivity is Power II: For Creative, Business, and Other Professionals – Hillary Rettig/1st edition,
ISBN 978-0-9899440-9-0 paperback
ISBN **979-8-9896387-0-3** ebook

To Jan Tobochnik

Contents

Vocabulary/Text Notes xi
On Using the Correct Toolset xiii
What to Do If You've Got an Urgent Deadline 1

PART I: EFFECTIVENESS 3
1. The Problem Isn't Laziness 5
   Sticking (or Not) to the Plan 8
2. The Problem Is Disempowerment 10
   Where the Disempowerment Comes From 11
   Family Disempowerments 12
   Societal Disempowerments 12
   "Life Events" Disempowerments 13
   Exercise 1 13
3. Procrastination and Perfectionism 15
   The Disempowerment Cascade 18
   Exercise 2 19
4. A Quick Solution to Procrastination: Reclaiming Your "Lost" Options and Outcomes 21
5. "Unproductive" Versus "Quasiproductive" Procrastination, and Other Distractions 24
   Debunking the Productivity Myths: "Good Procrastination," Multitasking, etc. 25
   Disconnecting Shouldn't Be Radical 26
6. Building Your *Sitzfleisch* 31
7. The Secret to Quantity *and* Quality 34
8. Working on the Right Stuff 38
9. The Re-Empowerment Process I: Overcoming Your Obstacles 40
   Table I: Sample Obstacle List for a Grant Writing Project 42
   Exercise 3 43
   Obstacle Resolution 44
   Table II: Sample Solutions List 44
   Exercise 4 46
10. The Re-Empowerment Process II. Why You Need to Ask for Help Early and Often 47
11. The Best Solution to Procrastination 49

PART II: COMPASSION 51
12. Perfectionist Myths and Realities 53
13. How Perfectionists Think 57
14. How Perfectionists Behave 64

Exercise 5 68
Exercise 6 69
15. Where We Learn Perfectionism 70
    The Parents' Trap 71
    Situational Perfectionism 72
    Exercise 7 73
16. Nonperfectionist Attitudes and Behaviors 74
    Exercise 8 79
17. The Three Most Important Things Nonperfectionists Know 80
18. The Nonperfectionist Mindset: Introducing Your Inner Compassionate Adult 83
    Reframing to Compassion 83
    Developing a Nonperfectionist Inner Monologue 85
    Exercise 9. Intentionally Erroneous Emails 87
    Exercise 10. Nonperfectionism Around the House, and in Your Daily Life 87
19. Interrupting the Disempowerment Cascade 89
    How to Stop Fighting Your Inner Perfectionist 91
20. Overcoming a Punishment Habit 92
    Exercise 11 93
21. How to Distinguish Between High Standards and Perfectionism ...95
22. Learning the Art of Failure 98
    Exercise 12 100
23. Learning the Art of Success 102
    The Costs of Success 104
    Exercise 13 105
24. Overcoming Ambivalence 106
    Solutions to Ambivalence 107
    Exercise 14 108

PART III: JOYFUL WORK 109
25. Introducing the Joyful Dance 111
    Get Random! 113
26. Speed It Up! 115
    Make Haste, Slowly 118
27. Get Fresh! 120
28. Wizard-Level Problem-Solving 122
29. How to Get, and Stay, Inspired 126
    Know Thyself and Thy Motivations 128
30. How to Write Like a Pro 130
31. Navigating the Project Life Cycle 135
    How to Handle "The Question" 137
    Exercise 15 139

32. Avoiding the "Big Four" Project Derailments 140
    Banish "Beginning Bias" and Other Avoidance-Related Problems 140
    Rein in Reckless Research 141
    Finish Off "Fear of Finishing" 142
    Give Boredom the Boot 142
    Exercise 16 144
33. How to Take Excellent Breaks 145

PART IV: RESILIENCE 149
34. The Many Forms of Criticism and Rejection 151
    Why It Hurts 152
    Exercise 17 154
35. How to Cope 156
36. Strategies for Difficult Conversations 161
    When You're the Critic 164
    Exercise 18 165
37. How to Stay Safe (and Productive) on Social Media 166
    For Those Posting Political Content 168

PART V: ABUNDANCE 171
38. An Awesome Liberation 173
39. What Makes a Good Time Manager 176
    Why Being Busy Isn't the Virtue Many People Think It Is 178
    Exercise 19 179
40. Investing Your Time 180
41. Shifting from Expenses to Investments 184
    Reining in Your Escapist Activities 185
    Getting Frugal 187
42. The Only Thing More Precious Than Your Time 190
    Exercise 20 191
43. Specialize! 193
44. The Joys of Declining and Delegating 196
45. The Perils of Overgiving 199
    Overcoming Email/Messaging/Collaborative Apps Overload 201
    About Boundaries 202
    Kids Rock! 203
    Exercise 21 205
    Exercise 22 205
46. Budgeting Your Time 206
    The Genius of Underscheduling 209
    Sample Weekly Time Budget 210
    Table III: Sample Weekly Time Budget for a Working Parent With Vocation .. 211

Exercise 23 211
47. Scheduling and Tracking Your Time 213
    Tracking.. 214
    Exercise 24 215
48. Putting It All Together 216

CONCLUSION: LIBERATING YOURSELF AND THE WORLD 221

Acknowledgments.. 227
If This Book Has Helped You... 228
About the Author.. 229

Vocabulary/Text Notes

Procrastination is the problem of not being able to reliably do your work as planned.

A block, as in "writer's block" or "creative block," is a severe, prolonged bout of procrastination.

When I need a verb form, I generally use "procrastinate," and my preferred adjective is "underproductive." In both cases, I'm referring to the entire spectrum of underproductivity, from slight procrastination to a severe block.

For reasons that will become clear, I avoid using labels like "procrastinator" and "perfectionist" in conversation or when teaching, but I do use them in this book for brevity and clarity.

I use descriptors like "productive" and "prolific" not to indicate some arbitrary standard of productivity, but someone working at their own comfortable-but-focused capacity. Ditto for "successful": I always use that to mean that you get a good result relative to your own situation and efforts.

I frequently distinguish between a job that you do entirely, or primarily, for money, and a "vocation" or "mission" that you do out of interest or passion. (Of course, some are lucky enough to be able to earn a living from their vocation, and if that's your goal, the techniques in this book will help.)

I don't distinguish between "creative" and "noncreative" work: it's all creative.

I use the term "mentor" as a catch-all for any kind of advisor, be they a teacher, coach, family member, coworker, colleague, supervisor, therapist, or friend. Hopefully, your life is filled with wise and kind mentors.

I use gender neutral pronouns (singular they/them) except when a person's pronouns are gendered, or when gendered pronouns are useful for clarity.

The case studies in this book are composites that reflect real-life situations. Many of the shorter anecdotes and examples, however, are true stories that happened pretty much as told, although I do change the names of those involved and other identifying details.

On Using the Correct Toolset

The techniques in this book have helped many, but no technique helps everyone, so feel free to skip any that aren't working for you. I'm unable to guarantee a positive result when using any of the techniques in this book.

Underproductivity often occurs alongside physical health problems (e.g., fatigue), mental health problems (e.g., anxiety or depression), a learning difference (e.g., dyslexia or ADHD), and/or neurodivergence. In these situations, my techniques can be useful adjuncts to medical or therapeutic treatment, but should not replace it. If you are dealing with one of these types of conditions, or even if you think you might be, please consult a specialist.

What to Do If You've Got an Urgent Deadline

This section is specifically for those who, right now, are facing an urgent deadline. If that's you, keep reading. If not, feel free to skip to Chapter 1. (I'll be covering all the points in more detail throughout the rest of the book.)

Here's what you should do if you're facing an urgent deadline:
1. **Clear your schedule.** Your most urgent needs right now are for time and energy, so make a list of everything you're supposed to be doing, including your job, work, community or other projects, family obligations, and personal chores and errands. Then, take a serious look at each item and ask yourself: "Is it essential that I do this **now**?"

    If the answer is "no," postpone it. (Or, if you don't have to do it at all, cancel it.)

    For projects that you absolutely must do, see if you can cancel or postpone any part of them.

    What about your self-care? (Sleep, grooming, exercise, medical and therapy appointments, etc.) Don't cut that: your health and well-being are important, and not just because they aid your productivity. Feel free, however, to postpone "optional" appointments like a haircut, and if you're doing an intensive daily athletic or other practice, you might want to skip a session or two.

    Your social life and recreation? Postpone or cancel most of your engagements, keeping just a few of the most fun. (We don't want you to get all isolated and cranky.)

    After you've finished, repeat the entire process and see if you can cut some more. (You often can.) Be relentless.

This process should liberate lots of time for your urgent project. Use two-thirds of it for the project, and the remaining third for some additional self-care and recreation.

2. **Ask for a deadline extension.** Your supervisor / teacher / editor / coworker / colleague might grant you one, especially if you're late for reasons beyond your control, like an illness. Ask sooner rather than later, however, because waiting till the last minute makes you look bad, and also leaves you working under unnecessary pressure and stress.

3. **Reduce your project's scope.** Meaning: figure out which parts you don't have to do, and eliminate them. Be ruthless! If writing a routine report for work, keep it short and stick to the essentials. If writing a blog post or other short expository piece, keep it focused on one or two major points. And if organizing a work or community event, also keep it focused, eliminating any optional program items or elements.

    If you know you won't be able to complete the project on time under any circumstances, then ask your supervisor, mentor, editor, coach, or other collaborator which project elements would be best to get done now, and which can wait. It's usually better to do a great job on four project elements than a mediocre job on six. (Sometimes, you can submit an outline or sketch of the unfinished elements.)

    After you've eliminated all the unnecessary elements from your project, start trimming bits and pieces. (They add up.) Do this cutting sooner rather than later, so you don't waste time working on stuff you cut later. If you're afraid of "overcutting," check with your supervisor, mentor, or other colleague. Chances are you'll be fine—especially since many people, and especially novices and perfectionists, tend to overstuff their projects. Finally:

4. **Read—or, at least, skim—Part III.** It's loaded with techniques that will help you accelerate your work.

Good luck! See you after you're done.

Part I

Effectiveness

1. The Problem Isn't Laziness

You've probably noticed how people don't like talking about it when things aren't going well. "How are you doing?" you ask. If the answer isn't "Great!" it's usually "Good." Or, at worst, "Okay."

Sometimes a friend will tell you about their relationship, job, health, or even, if you're really close, money problems. But there's one thing that people have trouble opening up about to even their closest friends, and that's their problems getting their work done. There seems to be something uniquely shameful about underproductivity. Yet, so many of us have been there:

- The endless days and nights when you know you should be working but are doing anything and everything but.
- The more-or-less constant feelings of guilt, shame, and fear.
- The lies. Such as telling yourself, "I'll work on it tonight," when you know you won't. And telling your friends, "I work best under pressure," when you know you don't. And telling your supervisor, editor, teacher, or colleague who is waiting for the project, "It's almost done," when you know it isn't.
- The frantic couple of days before—or after—your deadline, when your fear finally builds to the point where you start working. Being fear-driven, however, you feel no real attachment to the work, and are super distracted and inefficient.
- The death-march all-nighters when every second feels like you're dragging a heavy weight.
- The feeling of defeat when you finally hand the work in knowing it could have been so much better.

- And finally: the humiliation of getting a mediocre result and maybe a comment from your supervisor or colleague like, "Great idea, weak execution," or, "Were you rushed?"

The problem is procrastination. Everyone does it, at one time or another, so why all the secrecy and shame? It's probably because we misidentify the causes. **Many people think they procrastinate because they're lazy or undisciplined but that's wrong: we procrastinate because we haven't been taught the attitudes and habits of productive work.** Even worse, we've been taught some *anti*productive attitudes and habits, like perfectionism.

Here's an example:

Eric planned to get his master's degree in just eighteen months, which meant taking two classes at a time. This was on top of his full-time job, long commute, and busy social life, but he didn't anticipate any problems: he liked staying busy and considered himself well organized.

But things went awry from the start.

His classes turned out to be much more work than anticipated, with the reading alone taking at least a couple of hours a day. And it was difficult reading that he really had to focus on, so his plan of doing it during his crowded and distracting train commute was only partially successful.

He had also planned on studying during his lunch hours but that didn't work out so well, either. Whether he worked at his desk or down in the employee cafeteria there were constant interruptions.

Most importantly, he had planned on doing a solid three hours of schoolwork most weeknights. He hadn't anticipated how hard it would be to concentrate on technical material after a full day of doing the same at his job, however. And so, he frequently found himself procrastinating via text breaks, snack breaks, gaming, and other distractions.

Another problem was that, although most of his friends and family were supportive of his need to study, some weren't. "We never see you anymore!" was a common refrain—and it often worked, with a guilty Eric abandoning his evening's study plans to do something with the person. (To be honest, his work was going so badly he often welcomed the distraction.)

Weekends were supposed to be set aside for studying and assignments, but household chores, including shopping and cleaning, cut into that time.

To make matters even worse, just a couple of weeks after he had started his classes, his supervisor, Tasha, assigned him a big new project. Normally, he would have jumped at the interesting work and higher-visibility role. But now, already feeling overwhelmed, he could only pretend to be enthusiastic.

In the back of his mind was the growing sense that *I can't handle it all*. But whenever he found himself thinking that consciously, he immediately shut the thought down. He was raised to be ambitious and always do his best—in fact, he thought of himself as a "machine" who could take on any amount of work.

Then the blow fell: despite all his efforts and struggles, he got poor grades on his first couple of assignments. Eric wasn't just humiliated, he was appalled—and his motivation never recovered. Both professors suggested he attend some optional tutorials, and also invited him to meet to discuss his work, but due to a combination of shame and time-crunch, he didn't do either.

Eric now found it harder and harder to do his schoolwork. He started skipping classes and spending more and more time on social media, television, and gaming. Of course, he didn't give up without a fight: inwardly he harangued himself to "Get your act together!" and "Stop being lazy!" And whenever he thought of the tuition money he was wasting he felt sick to his stomach.

At first, the harangues and shame seemed to work—at least, they were enough to motivate him to pull an all-nighter or two right before an assignment was due. (Of course, he was exhausted and underproductive at work the next day, and his grade inevitably reflected the last-minute effort.) After a while, however, even the harangues weren't enough to motivate him. The only thing they did was make him feel miserable.

Meanwhile, he was getting further and further behind, not just in his schoolwork but at his job.

Eric knew that, from the outside at least, he looked productive. He was always rushing from place to place, and constantly complaining (in a joking way, of course) about his "ridiculous" schedule and "monster" to-do list. More and more, however, he found himself, if not exactly lying, then shading the truth so as to not reveal his difficulties to others. He knew some people weren't fooled—not his professors and not Tasha, his supervisor, who for the first time ever had expressed disappointment at his work performance. (Eric had gotten off to a poor start with the new project.) But he felt he had no choice but to keep up the pretense.

By the end of the first semester, Eric had a strong sense that he wasn't going to be able to complete his degree. Unwilling to admit that to himself, much less to others, however, he enrolled for an additional expensive semester. By the end of that second semester, he knew he had to quit his degree program. It was a fresh humiliation to have to admit to others that he had failed, but also a relief to no longer have to keep up the pretense.

Fortunately, most people were understanding, although a few clueless ones said things like, "You should have planned better." Some encouraged him to try for his degree again when his job was less pressured—this time, taking just one class at a time.

But Eric didn't know if he would. He felt that his shame and disappointment would live on forever.

(To be continued...)

When you're stuck the way poor Eric was stuck, the situation can seem hopeless. But it isn't. The first step to solving the problem is understanding the true nature of that complicated phenomenon we call "procrastination."

Sticking (or Not) to the Plan

Many people start the day with a plan. Maybe you write yours out in a planner, or keep it all in your head. It could be something like this: wake up at 7:30 a.m., be at work by 9:00, go to gym during your lunch hour, etc.

Let's start, then, with a simple definition: **procrastination is when you get derailed from the plan or path you had intended to follow for the day.**[1] So, instead of getting up at 7:30, you get up at 8:00 or 8:30, or later.

Or, instead of doing the work you're supposed to be doing in the morning, you get distracted by unnecessary busy work or someone else's project. (Or, water-cooler gossip or social media.)

Or, instead of going to the gym, you spent your lunch hour doing the work you should have been doing all morning.

The key question is: what's derailing you? Often, we have a quick answer to that: "Me! I'm derailing myself because I'm lazy, undisciplined, uncommitted, etc." Not so fast! If you're like many people, you would do anything not to procrastinate, and have been trying for years to break the habit. So it's pretty clear that you're not really in charge.

I'll tell you who the "derailer" is in Chapter 11. For now, though, let's take a closer look at the phenomenon of procrastination, starting with five crucial points:

1. Procrastination always has a cause, and it's not us. We know this because many people who procrastinate do so mostly in one or two crucial areas, like work (or even just one work project) or exercise. Mean-

---

[1] And a "block," as in "writer's block" or "creative block," is a serious and sustained bout of procrastination. As mentioned in the Vocabulary/Text Notes, I mostly use the words "procrastination" and "block" interchangeably.

while, they're dynamos everywhere else. (Including, sometimes, helping others with the same types of work they themselves are avoiding.) It's clear, therefore, that they're not generally lazy, undisciplined, or uncommitted, but simply facing some additional barriers around those particular tasks.

2. Our reasons for procrastinating are always valid. There are many reasons you might not feel like doing your work, including fatigue, illness, boredom, confusion, overwhelm, and distraction. These are all 100% legitimate—meaning, understandable, forgivable, and human—and so are the more frivolous-seeming reasons, like that it's nice out and you want to spend the day outdoors, or that you're lonely and want to hang out with a friend.

The problem, in other words, isn't that you don't feel like working, but how you respond to that feeling. Which brings us to...

3. Procrastination isn't a sin or character flaw, but a suboptimal response to our obstacles and barriers to doing our work.[2] We all procrastinate sometimes, and a little procrastination isn't going to hurt you. But if our reflexive response to every obstacle we encounter is to procrastinate, then we've got a problem, because most of us encounter dozens or hundreds of obstacles every day. (More on obstacles in Chapter 9.)

4. You can't punish yourself out of a procrastination problem. Think about it: if punishments—like shame, guilt, and deprivation—actually worked, wouldn't we all be super achievers by now? Most procrastinators have been punishing themselves, or been punished by others, for years, with zero effect except that the problem got worse.

5. You can solve it, though. In fact, I'm going to give you a whole bunch of really effective solutions. Implement them, and you can achieve the central goal of productivity work, which is to be able to work as easily, effectively, and joyfully as possible within the limits of whatever constraints you may be facing. This goal actually encompasses two others: (a) the ability to optimize your use of your time, skills, energy, cognitive capacity (Chapter 42), and other resources; and (b) the ability to show up on time and do whatever work you're supposed to be doing with a high degree of clarity, engagement, focus, and fun. (Because we all need fun, and fun is motivating.)

First, however, let's discuss the true cause of procrastination.

---

[2] I mostly use the words "obstacle" and "barrier" interchangeably. However, when such a distinction is useful, I use "obstacle" to refer to "mostly internal" constraints like perfectionism, and "barrier" to "mostly external" ones like a lack of financial or other resources.

2. The Problem Is Disempowerment

Why would someone with a strong record of delivering projects on time suddenly find themselves unable to meet a work deadline?

Why is it sometimes easier to help others with their work than it is to do your own? (Even if it's the same type of work!)

Why can you get excited over a project when you happen to think about it away from your desk, but that excitement is nowhere to be found when you actually sit down to do it?

And why, when you sit down to watch television or play a video game "for just a few minutes," do you often wind up doing it for hours?

The answer, in all cases, is **disempowerment**: the state of being unable to use your strengths, skills, talents, knowledge, energy, enthusiasm, and other capacities. Some people exist in a state of general disempowerment, which means that they aren't able to get much of anything important done, while others are mostly disempowered in one or two key areas or around one or two key projects.

As you will see, there are many situations, circumstances, and conditions that can disempower us. But how, exactly, does disempowerment cause procrastination? And how can the situation be remedied? To answer these important questions, you first need to understand that **our work is really an act of self-expression, self-assertion, and self-advocacy.** Whenever you share your work with others, you're revealing yourself at a pretty deep level. (Your thoughts, ideas, values, vision, voice, etc.) Self-expression and sharing almost always carry some risk because you're exposing your ideas—and sometimes yourself—to criticism, judgment, and rejection.

2. The Problem Is Disempowerment

Even when delivered sensitively, that criticism, etc., can hurt. But if it's delivered cruelly or unjustly, as it often is, it can hurt a lot more. (More on this in Chapter 34.)

We procrastinate, in large part, to avoid that hurt. If you don't hand your work in, after all, it—and, by extension, you—can't be criticized or rejected. And even if you do manage to hand it in, procrastination provides a built-in justification for any disappointing outcomes you receive: "I was rushed." The problem is that, at the same time procrastination is keeping you safe from potential critics, it's also **isolating** you from, and thus rendering you **invisible** to, your essential audiences, including not just whoever is waiting for the work, but helpers, mentors, collaborators, and appreciators of all sorts. At its core, procrastination is a form of **self-silencing** and, sometimes, **self-censorship** (if you're specifically silencing ideas you think will offend, or be rejected by, others). It can also be a form of **hiding**—and sadly, because your rushed work doesn't reflect your best efforts, it's often the best part of you, and the best of your ideas, that you're hiding.

Finally, procrastination is also often **hoarding**. "I'll hand in my work when it's ready," the procrastinator thinks—only, it never is. Or, "I'll hand it in after this last set of changes"—only, the "last set" leads to another, and another, and another. Or, even worse, "I know I need help with this project, but I need to get it in a little better shape before I show it to someone." But the need to get it "in a little better shape" never ends. (More on hoarding in Chapter 14.)

Isolation, invisibility, self-silencing, self-censorship, hiding, and hoarding are all highly disempowered responses to the risks of self-expression, and the "safety" they offer comes at a high price: self-sabotage. Fortunately, there are more empowering responses to the risks, which I'll be discussing throughout this book.

Where the Disempowerment Comes From

Generally speaking, there are three main sources of disempowerment-based procrastination: your family, society, and certain life events. I discuss each below.

Family Disempowerments

Research has linked procrastination to "untreated traumatic experiences"[3] and authoritarian—i.e., harsh and controlling—parenting. In the latter case, psychologist Timothy Pychyl notes that procrastination, "may become one of the few means available to rebel against this [parental] control, a form of passive aggression."[4] I'll be revisiting this idea of procrastination as rebellion in Chapter 11.

In her book *Adult Children of Emotionally Immature Parents*, psychologist Lindsay Gibson notes how insecure and controlling parents tend to discourage their children's self-expression, including their abilities to speak their truth and ask for help. At the same time, these parents tend to encourage "uncertainty and self-doubt," "guilt and shame over imperfections," and "stereotyped gender roles." Make no mistake: these children are being taught to silence themselves and hide their true selves—and absent some healing therapy or mentoring, the need to do so will likely persist into adulthood, often resulting in a procrastination problem.

Societal Disempowerments

You don't have to have had a difficult childhood to be disempowered, however. Perfectionism, which I discuss in the next chapter and extensively in Part II, is highly disempowering, and it's rampant throughout our culture and media. You can also be disempowered by an ineffective work process (Part III), unhealed traumatic rejections (Part IV), or unmanaged time (Part V). And yeah: it's usually several of those happening at once.

On top of all this, many groups—including women, people of color, queer people, people with disabilities, poor people, and immigrants—experience **systemic oppression** and **implicit bias.** Generally speaking, the former is when an organization's policies intentionally or unintentionally lead to unequal outcomes for members of marginalized groups, while the latter is when the organization's policies aren't explicitly biased, but its members' attitudes and behaviors are. Some organizations have worked hard to eliminate the former problem, but the latter remains prevalent (perhaps because

---

[3] https://www.hazeldenbettyford.org/articles/fcd/teen-mental-health
[4] https://www.psychologytoday.com/us/blog/dont-delay/200903/parenting-style-and-procrastination. Psychologists commonly recognize four general parenting styles: authoritarian (lots of rules and control, little affection and support), indulgent (few rules, lots of affection), neglectful (few rules, little affection), and authoritative (lots of rules, lots of affection). Authoritative is considered best.

policies are easier to change than people's attitudes). If you're a member of a targeted group, you unfortunately have the added, unjust burden of learning how to recognize and cope with barriers such as discrimination, harassment, stereotype threat, tokenization, and microaggressions. It's a shame that you would have to do such extra work, but coping always beats noncoping, a.k.a., procrastination.

Our final source of disempowerment is...

"Life Events" Disempowerments.

Some life events can also be disempowering. Obviously, the "bad" ones, such as an illness, job loss, or relationship breakup, can be, but even "good" ones, such as a wonderful new job or relationship, can also be, at least temporarily. Transitions—e.g., from one project, job, or career to another—are inherently disempowering. True, the "good" disempowerments will often spur your intellectual, creative, social, and emotional growth. But you still have to be able to cope with them.

Exercise 1

Make a list of any transitional obstacles you're currently facing, and journal* about how each is affecting you and your ability to do your work. While writing, also take some time to appreciate how you've persevered—including by reading this book—in the face of all those obstacles.

*Whenever, in this book, I talk about journaling, I mean "free writing," also known as "stream of consciousness writing." Start with a question like, "How has taking this new job [or moving to a new town, etc.] affected me and my work?" Then take your time writing out as complete an answer as you can. Let the words flow and don't worry about spelling, punctuation, or grammar: you're not showing this to anyone. The goal isn't fabulous prose, but introspection: a better, clearer, more comprehensive introspection than you can achieve just by thinking about the problem. Just remember to always write in a problem-solving way (e.g., "I can see at least three ways that the transition is affecting me...") and *never* in a shaming or blaming way ("I'm lazy, that's all!"). Always be your own best coach.

If you're worried that this journaling, or any of the exercises in this book, can themselves become a form of procrastination—or, more specifically, what I call Quasiproductive Procrastination (Chapter 5)—don't be: these exercises are specifically designed to help you feel more empowered around your work; and the more empowered you feel, the more you'll be able to get back to your work, and the sooner you'll want to.

Please do Exercise 1, and every exercise in this book, with as much energy and attention as you can. In the realm of personal growth, halfway measures usually don't get us far. (In fact, they're likely to be counterproductive, yielding all the pains and inconveniences of the effort with few or none of the rewards.) But putting your heart and soul into the quest can be transformational.

3. Procrastination and Perfectionism

In the last chapter, I discussed how a disempowering desire to self-silence or hide is often at the root of procrastination; also how our disempowerment can arise from our childhood, society, or life events. But how is it that some who have experienced significant disempowerment can still manage to be productive? And why do so many who haven't experienced it still wind up procrastinating? Great questions! Let's answer them one at a time.

On the question of why some people are productive despite having had a disempowering childhood, or having endured other disempowering circumstances, please keep in mind that, just as procrastination always has a cause (or causes), so does productivity. Maybe the person was privileged and had the resources, like money and family connections, to overcome their barriers. Or, maybe they weren't that privileged, but had one or two key people who supported and mentored them. Or, maybe they had excellent skills in one or two key areas—technical, interpersonal, strategic, or otherwise—that helped them to break through. Or maybe they were lucky in some other way. (Most likely, they were lucky in several ways.)

As to the question of why so many who haven't experienced serious personal disempowerment still procrastinate, there are three answers. First, procrastination is strongly habit-forming. Every time you do it, even if only for superficial reasons like boredom or distraction, you become a little more disempowered and fearful around your work, thus making it harder to do that work in the future. In some cases, procrastination probably crosses the line into an actual addiction—generally defined as a self-reinforcing or compulsive behavior with negative consequences. Hard as it is to overcome a habit, it's even harder to overcome an addiction.[5]

Second—and recalling that procrastination is often used as a way of hiding from possible negative reactions to ourselves and our ideas—even many seemingly neutral or benign tasks actually do have a scary, self-revealing component. If you have a lifelong dream of being an artist or performer, or of learning a foreign language (possibly as a prelude to living abroad), or of starting a small business, then taking even a small step in that direction, like signing up for a class, can raise the kinds of fears that lead to procrastination. (The proof is that so many people have these kinds of dreams but never act on them.) Then there's the risk of getting criticized—sometimes passive-aggressively in the form of teasing—by friends and family. (When someone reacts negatively to your taking a growth step, it's likely because they feel guilty or defensive about their own choices—and not a good sign for your relationship.)

Finally: even many activities that most people admit are legitimately scary or stressful—like, looking for work[6] or online dating—are actually much scarier and more stressful when you're in the midst of them than even many sympathetic onlookers understand. So, we can wind up more fearful than anticipated, and with a consequent stronger need to procrastinate. (Again, if someone is trivializing or otherwise unsupportive of your experience, that's more a reflection on them than you, and not a good sign.)

Please note that even a small amount of disempowerment can trigger procrastination, especially if we've got other stresses going on in our life. Worse still, if we happen to confide in someone about our challenges, we're often told to, "Stop whining!" "Stop complaining!" "Toughen up!" or, "Get over it!" This mentality is deeply perfectionist, which brings us to the third reason why even people who haven't faced serious personal disempowerment can have trouble working: **perfectionism**. It's probably the most disempowering force in many people's lives, not just because it's ubiquitous in our culture and media (more on that in Chapter 15), but because, along with being a barrier in its own right, it also blocks your ability to solve your other

---

[5] Some experts do indeed believe that procrastination has much in common with "classic" addictions like alcoholism. See, for instance,
https://www.cambridge.org/core/journals/behavioral-and-brain-sciences/article/abs/addiction-procrastination-and-failure-points-in-decisionmaking-systems/2255C0E5BE4D6A86ED9BE92646EE5819#.

[6] My book It's Not You, It's Your Strategy: Finding Work in a Tough Job Market can help. Download it for free, in English or Spanish, here: HTTPs.

problems. It does that not just by making you think that you're lazy or otherwise "the problem" (as discussed earlier), but by swamping you with guilt and shame, emotions that aren't exactly conducive to problem-solving.

To sum up: perfectionism can cause you to procrastinate even in the absence of an authoritarian childhood or other instigating factors. Conversely, if someone is lucky enough to not be too perfectionist, they'll have an easier time coping with any barriers they might be facing.

Perfectionism is a complex phenomenon, and I discuss it in detail in Part II. For now, all you need to know is that it creates not just a fear of failure, but a terror of it. Many perfectionist characteristics, including the tendencies to: (a) define success narrowly and unrealistically, and (b) try to use punishment (e.g., harsh self-talk and deprivation) as a corrective or motivator, contribute to that terror. But the biggest contributor is probably that **perfectionists overidentify with their work**. To a perfectionist, every "success" is a source of personal validation, and every "failure" a devastating indictment. (I frequently put quotation marks around those words to indicate that they are relative terms, and also that perfectionists often misuse them. See below, and also Chapters 22 and 23.)

But wait! It can get even worse, because **perfectionists also constantly see themselves as failing**. Even at times when they've succeeded. (E.g., "An A- is okay, I guess, but I'm really bummed I didn't get an A.") That means that, because of their constant overidentification, they are also constantly in despair. This double-punch of negativity (devaluation of you and your work) and overidentification can also lead you to be constantly judging, evaluating, and critiquing both your work and yourself, all in a desperate, and exhausting, effort to stave off the inevitable "failures."

Overidentification can also manifest itself as:

- **Pathologizing**, meaning that you interpret ordinary work obstacles and setbacks as a sign you're incapable of doing the work. Example: "It took me forever to find the bugs in my program, so I guess I'm just terrible at programming." (And that "forever" exemplifies not just hyperbole, but also shortsightedness and impatience, perfectionist characteristics I discuss in Chapters 13 and 14.)
- An **overemphasis on external recognition and rewards**—so that, for instance, a good outcome or a compliment from your friend or colleague (or even a stranger) can put you over the moon. (And the obverse: an even slightly critical one can ruin your day.)
- **Using your work as a source of self-worth or legitimacy.** "If I could only achieve X, then I would finally be Y," is a common perfectionist formulation. Example: "If I could only get published, then

I would finally be a 'real' writer." Let's be clear: the goal (in this case, publication) is often fine and admirable. The problem is when your sense of self-worth or legitimacy hinges on it. (Also note the use of the perfectionist intensifier: "finally.")

When you encounter someone who is generally productive but is procrastinating a lot on one or two key projects, you can bet they're overidentified with those projects.

The Disempowerment Cascade

Perfectionism triggers procrastination in a five-step process I call the **Disempowerment Cascade**. Here are the steps:
1. While working, or attempting to work, you encounter one or (usually) more obstacles (confusion, boredom, distraction, overwhelm, fatigue, etc.).
2. You have a presentiment of failure. "Oh no!" you think. "My work's not going well! I'm going to fail!" Please note that you're often afraid of failing not just at the current work session, but at the entire project—and even at your job, career, life, etc. That's a lot of fear. So, naturally…
3. You panic. Which then leads you to…
4. Urgently attempt to get yourself back on track. Unfortunately, most procrastinators know only one way to do this, a harsh and shaming inner monologue that goes something like this:
    "What's wrong with you? Why are you so lazy? This stuff isn't hard. Anyone could do it! Amy's already finished. Why can't you be disciplined like her? C'mon! If you don't get to work, you're gonna fail and everyone's gonna know you're a loser…and did I mention that the stuff you've already done sucks?"
    I'll have a lot more to say about this monologue later, but for now let's just agree that all it does is add fear on top of fear. And so, eventually, your panic rises to the point where you must…
5. Escape ("derail") via procrastination. You start scrolling on your phone, or bust out a video game, or even do some tedious chores. (Because anything's better than facing your work, and the terrifying prospect of failure.)

Those are the steps—and it's important to note that they can happen at any point while you're working, or even before you start working. (In which case, you probably won't even start.) All five steps can, and usually do, happen in a flash, so that you might not even be aware of them. All you know is that you have a sudden, irresistible urge to do something—anything—other than your work.

The Disempowerment Cascade model shows that it's not the obstacles (confusion, boredom, etc.) that are the barrier to productivity, but our terrorized reaction to them. When we're terrified, we lose capacity—which happens to be the definition of disempowerment, remember? That's why the only "solution" we can come up with is the unsatisfactory one of procrastination.

The Disempowerment Cascade model suggests two key differences between productive and underproductive people:

1. *Productive people learn to interrupt the Disempowerment Cascade.* Specifically, they replace the "panicking" step with problem-solving, with the goal of eliminating, or at least minimizing, the obstacle that is causing the derailment. This enables them to return to work as soon as possible.
2. *Productive people learn to minimize occurrences of the Disempowerment Cascade.* They do this by dealing definitively—or as definitively as possible—with their obstacles, so that they are either minimized or eliminated. If a productive person's workspace is noisy or uncomfortable, for instance, they'll quickly find a better one, and be more selective in the future. Or, if they get derailed after receiving an upsetting text message, they'll decide that, from that moment on, they won't check their phone until after they've done their work. **To outsiders, it looks like these productive people have phenomenal willpower, but what they're really doing is constantly removing obstacles to their productivity.**

Meanwhile, the underproductive people—who, let's not forget, are convinced that they themselves are the problem—tend not to recognize their true obstacles. This means, of course, that they are unlikely to be able to solve them.

And so those obstacles just keep reoccurring, and often get worse over time.

Exercise 2

Think back on a time when you were procrastinating and describe the roles that disempowerment and perfectionism played in that procrastination.

PRODUCTIVITY IS POWER II

Then describe how disempowerment, procrastination, and perfectionism can all cause each other and be caused by each other.

4. A Quick Solution to Procrastination: Reclaiming Your "Lost" Options and Outcomes

Disempowerment often misleads us into thinking that we have fewer and worse **options** than we really have. Maybe you think, for instance, that your only options for a project are to "be a fantastic success" or "be a total failure." Even if you do have a decent shot at that success, you're still putting huge pressure on yourself.

To be clear, people rarely frame it exactly that way to themselves because when you do, it sounds, well, silly. But often we're holding onto such a vision of success in the back of our mind. "Get an A or die trying" and "failure is not an option," are classic perfectionist formulations—and even when we say them jokingly, we kinda, sorta half mean them. But the vision could also be, "I want to write the great American novel" or,"I want to change the world" or, "I want to make millions from my small business by the time I'm thirty"—all with the unspoken add on, "...and if I don't succeed at that, I'm a loser."

Don't get me wrong: I'm all for ambitious goals and high standards, especially when backed by a good strategic plan. But as I'll discuss in Chapter 21, perfectionism is when you cross the line into improbable or even impossible goals. Also, the above modes of thinking all reflect an overemphasis on product over process, external recognition and rewards over internal ones, grandiosity, and other perfectionist attitudes. (See Chapter 13.)

Here are some examples of perceived poor options:

- Marci feels stuck having to choose between a career she loves but that doesn't pay well (music) and one that she is less enthusiastic about but that does pay well (engineering).

- Chris feels that, because one of their coworkers on a project is slacking off, they're stuck either having to do more than their fair share of the work, or getting a bad result.
- Oliver feels like he must either stay in a bad romantic relationship or be doomed to loneliness.

Disempowered people also often perceive themselves as having only poor potential **outcomes**: meaning that, no matter how hard they work on a project, or how carefully they navigate a situation, they are doomed to failure. This often leads to feelings of hopelessness and futility, arguably the most disempowering emotions of all. (As the Star Trek Borg, who are constantly pointing out to their would-be victims that, "resistance is futile," surely know.) Psychologists call the act of anticipating terrible outcomes *catastrophizing*, and many underproductive people do it a lot. They may think they're being "realistic" or "prepared for the worst," but what they're really doing is being negative (see Chapter 13) and disempowering themselves.

Please note that, even though I've been talking a lot about feelings and perceptions, I'm *not* saying that the actual obstacles—poor musician pay, a slacking coworker, and a bad relationship—aren't real and serious. Of course they are. The perceptual problem lies in believing that you have worse options and outcomes than you actually have. Catastrophizing can lead you to do this, and so can **dichotomizing**, another common perfectionist behavior in which you see the world in either/or terms. Notice how all of the above examples are dichotomized, with Marci feeling like she must choose between a career she loves and one that pays well, Chris feeling like they must choose between either doing more than their fair share of the work or handing in a bad project, and Oliver feeling like he's stuck between staying in a bad relationship or being lonely.

Like all perfectionism, negativity and dichotomization can shut your motivation right down. And so, **whenever you're feeling unmotivated, a good technique is to take a break from whatever it is you're trying to do and either journal about the problem or talk it over with someone, with the goal of creating better options and outcomes for yourself.** Once you do that, you should find your motivation returning.

Back to our examples:

Instead of feeling stuck having to choose between a career she loves (music) and one that pays well (engineering), Marci could: (1) choose a career spanning both fields, such as audio engineering, (2) pursue a musical career ultra-professionally so as to have the best chance of success, and/or,

4. A Quick Solution to Procrastination: Reclaiming Your "Lost" Options and Outcomes

(3) pursue an engineering career in a way that supports her music. (For instance, getting a job in a "music town" like New Orleans, Seattle, or Chicago; then (4) working a four-day week so she has long weekends to devote to her music.)

Instead of feeling stuck between either having to do more than their fair share of the work or handing in a bad project, Chris could, (1) talk with their coworker. (They might be unaware of the problem, or doing more than Chris realizes, or have a valid or easily correctable reason for underproducing.) Or Chris could, (2) ask their supervisor to assign them another collaborator. Or, they could even cut their losses and: (3) settle for the worse outcome (if the project isn't that important), or (4) just go ahead and do the extra work (if it is).

Instead of feeling stuck between either a bad relationship or a life of loneliness, Oliver could: (1) schedule more time with friends, (2) join a club or other organization where he'll meet new people, and/or (3) do some online dating. Or, if he feels the relationship is fixable, he could try to (4) get some relationship counseling.

In each case, we've gone from two bad options (and the associated bad outcomes) to four better ones—and whenever you use this technique, you should achieve a similar result. What you're really doing when you use this technique is re-empowering yourself. **If disempowerment is the state of being unable to access your strengths, skills, talents, knowledge, and other capacities, empowerment is the ability to access and use all of those.** Happily, as the above examples illustrate, shifting from one to the other state often comes down to a simple willingness to try to come up with some new options and outcomes.

Please note: I am *not* saying that the above solutions are easy, perfect, or even fair—only that they are all way better than procrastinating, which solves nothing and usually makes things worse. Besides, life can, and often does, surprise you. Especially once you've used this book's techniques to free yourself from the yoke of perfectionism, ineffective work processes, traumatic rejections, and unmanaged time, your options may, in fact, turn out to be much better than anticipated. As writer adrienne maree brown says in her book *Emergent Strategy*, "Creating more possibilities is...where we shape tomorrow towards abundance."

5. "Unproductive" Versus "Quasiproductive" Procrastination, and Other Distractions

People procrastinate in two main ways: "unproductively" and "quasiproductively."

Unproductive Procrastination (UP) is when, instead of your scheduled work, you do a low-value activity like social media, gaming, or television. (Yes, they can sometimes be high value, but often they're not, especially if you're using them to procrastinate.)

Quasiproductive Procrastination (QP) is when, instead of your scheduled work, you do an activity that has some value. It could be other, less urgent work. Or you could go for a run, do some chores, or do a favor for a friend.

QP is sneakier than UP because it gives you the illusion of being productive. "Well, I didn't get my work done today, but at least I got in a run," you tell yourself. Or, "at least I cleaned up the place." Or, "at least I helped a friend." Also, others will encourage your QP. The other runners will give you props for your dedication, your family or housemates will be glad that you cleaned, and your friend will be grateful for the help.

A common, and extra-sneaky, form of QP is when you procrastinate on one part of your project by overworking another. Examples include the very common problems of: (a) researching your novel or thesis to death but never actually getting around to writing it, and (b) endlessly revising it but never handing it in. Similarly, I've known entrepreneurs who lovingly imagined every detail of their artwork or jewelry designs, or how their boutique or other retail business should look, but never managed to get around to writing their business plan. Others labored over the text part

5. "Unproductive" Versus "Quasiproductive" Procrastination, and Other Distractions

of their plan, but balked at doing the profit & loss statement, balance sheet, and other financial projections, which are really the heart of the thing. (Michael E. Gerber's classic entrepreneurial guide, *The E-Myth Revisited*, is helpful in distinguishing between "having a passion," and "building a business around that passion.")

Other forms of QP include overoptimizing (a.k.a., "letting the perfect be the enemy of the good enough"), ambivalence (which I discuss in Chapter 24), indecision, and "overthinking the problem" a.k.a. "analysis paralysis."[7]

As the 20th century humorist Robert Benchley put it, "Anyone can do any amount of work, provided it isn't the work he is supposed to be doing at that moment."

So how do you know when you're doing QP? First, remember that, as discussed in Chapter 1, the goal of productivity work is to be able to stick to your plan. So, if you had planned to do X, but are now doing Y, and Y is at least somewhat useful, there's a good chance you're doing QP.

Also, we usually do know, deep down, when we're procrastinating. So, learn to listen for, and to, that small voice in your head that's saying, "I really ought to be doing something else."

Finally, overdo a QP activity enough and it will eventually become UP—and then you'll really know you're wasting time.

Debunking the Productivity Myths: "Good Procrastination," Multitasking, etc.[8]

Every once in a while, some expert claims that procrastination is "thinking time," and therefore useful. Or, that you can "productively procrastinate" on a big, scary task by doing lots of little, unscary ones instead. (Yup, they're actually recommending QP.) Or, they offer some other rationale or justification for procrastination. Repeat after me: **there's no such thing as "good procrastination."** (Or "positive" or "productive" procrastination.)

---

[7] Like this cat: https://youtu.be/p_17nvsuFFA.
[8] Citations for this discussion: Can't concentrate on more than one complicated task: https://sloanreview.mit.edu/article/the-impossibility-of-focusing-on-two-things-at-once/. Interruptions are expensive: https://www.npr.org/2015/09/22/442582422/the-cost-of-interruptions-they-waste-more-time-than-you-think. Social media degrades cognitive capacity of those around you:
https://en.wikipedia.org/wiki/Cognitive_load#college_students; cell phones degrade cognitive capacity even when not used: https://hbr.org/2018//03/having-your-smartphone-nearby-takes-a-toll-on-your-thinking.

Procrastination is always grounded in disempowerment, and disempowerment is never good.

I'm sure the people promoting these kinds of ideas are doing so in good faith—and while I'm happy that they've found a solution that works for them, that doesn't mean you should assume it will work for you.

Similarly, every few years, multitasking (working on more than one thing at a time) gets hyped as a productivity technique. But it's really a sham, for at least three reasons: (a) most of us can't concentrate on more than one complicated task at a time—and when we try, our efficiency goes way down; (b) it takes way more time to get back up to speed after an interruption than most people realize; and (c) multitasking can lead to QP by encouraging you to focus on your easier tasks at the expense of your harder ones.

So don't multitask.

And while I'm at it: don't mix work and social media. Research has shown that you can't work effectively while keeping one eye on your feed—which shouldn't be surprising, since social media platforms are literally designed to hijack your attention. In fact, the social media designers are so very good at their jobs that research has shown that just having your phone visible, *even if you're not actually using it*, degrades not just your own productivity but that of the people sitting near you. That's pretty incredible—and also a good reason to leave your phone in your bag—or, better yet, another room—while working.

Be careful when listening to music while working. While some people can work with music in the background, many can't.

Another way to put all of the above is: don't be what productivity expert Cal Newport, in his book *How to Become a Straight-A Student,* calls a "pseudo-worker." "The pseudo-worker looks and feels like someone who is working hard—he or she spends a long time in the library and is not afraid to push on late into the night—but, because of a lack of focus and concentration, doesn't actually accomplish that much."

You may be the cosmic exception to all this: the rare person who can really multitask, or work effectively while also using social media. But you're probably not—and if you get this wrong, you're at risk for some serious self-sabotage.

Disconnecting Shouldn't Be Radical

One of productivity work's big divides is between those who try to work while connected to the Internet and its many distractions and those who have figured out that that's a really bad idea. The second group understands

5. "Unproductive" Versus "Quasiproductive" Procrastination, and Other Distractions

the benefits of disconnecting at least part of the time, including not just increased productivity, but less stress, better health, and more enjoyment of life in general.[9]

Yes, I know that you need to be on the Internet sometimes. But you probably don't need to be on it as much as you think. You can, for instance, organize your work so that you do all your online tasks together in a batch, thus freeing you to disconnect for a while. And you can also train yourself to save minor online tasks—like looking up a date or writing a quick email—for your next online session, instead of constantly letting them interrupt your flow. (I keep some scratch paper near my computer so that I can write down such tasks as they occur to me.)

Another great technique is to download lectures and other videos so that you can listen to them offline. Doing this also gives you more flexibility, such as the ability to listen to lectures while driving or on the bus.

Ditto for reference materials: if you think you'll need certain formulas or constants to do your work, then download that information and organize it into a document before starting.

Even many people who think they must be online constantly for their work can cut back some—and often a lot. After writer and consultant Gregory Ferenstein started using timers to limit his social media use, for instance, he realized that:

> [T]here was hardly ever a time when I needed to constantly monitor social media. Even when I posted something that was popular, I rarely needed to spend more time than a few minutes on the app to meaningfully engage. The marginal utility [meaning, the additional value] from minutes 5 to 60 on Facebook and Twitter wasn't much more than the first 5 minutes.[10]

You don't hear much about it, but many people do disconnect regularly. (Again, see the links in Footnote 10.) Some only go online in the afternoons or evenings after finishing their work; while others limit email and other online work to just once or twice a day; while still others shun certain applications—e.g., some social media platforms—entirely. Still others abstain on weekends or do multiday "digital detox" retreats. Novelists Zadie Smith, Isabel Allende, and Jonathan Franzen are famous "disconnecters,"

---

[9] See, for instance: https://www.insidehighered.com/blogs/gradhacker/how-killing-your-home-internet-can-boost-your-productivity, https://www.theminimalists.com/internet/, and http://blogs.publishersweekly.com/blogs/shelftalker/?p=5127

[10] https://www.forbes.com/sites/gregoryferenstein/2019/01/31/how-i-cut-my-social-media-use-with-app-limits/

and so is Cal Newport, who's written two books on the topic: *Digital Minimalism* and *A World Without Email*. Programming legend Donald Knuth is a disconnecting pioneer and in 1990 famously explained his decision to almost entirely dispense with email this way: "Email is a wonderful thing for people whose role in life is to be on top of things. But not for me; my role is to be on the bottom of things. What I do takes long hours of working and uninterruptible concentration."[11]

Let's be clear, however, that even many who need to "be on top of things"—like, say, many activists or entrepreneurs—benefit from limiting their time online, both because their work does indeed have an intellectual or creative component that requires sustained concentration, and also because a lot of our online time is spent on low-value activities like social media and watching videos. Of course it's okay to do some of that. (And I allocate some time for it in Chapter 46's sample time budget and schedule.) But too much is problematic, not just from a productivity and effectiveness standpoint, but a mental and physical health standpoint.[12]

If all this sounds extreme, please remember that the choice isn't a dichotomized "always online" versus "always offline" one: it's about seeing the Internet and social media as the tools that they are and figuring out how best to use them. It's especially about recognizing that the apps are designed by experts to suck you in, and that being sucked in is actually a form of disempowerment that, like all forms of disempowerment, you want to avoid. By the way, that "sucked in" experience has a name: a **ludic loop**. The classic ludic-loop-generating technology is the slot machine, which uses fun and flashy displays—plus the lure of the occasional small win and the possibility of an (extremely rare) big win—to hook people and suck their time and money out of them. But many social media apps, television shows, games, and other escapist diversions are also designed to generate ludic loops. (In

---

[11] https://www.calnewport.com/blog/2008/07/17/bonus-post-how-the-worlds-most-famous-computer-scientist-checks-e-mail-only-once-every-three-months/

[12] Mental health: See, for instance, research conducted by psychologist Melissa G. Hunt and colleagues on undergraduates that found a causal link between time spent on Facebook, Instagram, and Snapchat, and feelings of depression and loneliness. https://penntoday.upenn.edu/news/social-media-use-increases-depression-and-loneliness. And also see Chapter 17 and the citations listed in Footnote #35. Physical health: See, for example: http://www.mayoclinic.org/healthy-lifestyle/adult-health/expert-answers/sitting/faq-20058005,
http://www.ncbi.nlm.nih.gov/pmc/articles/PMC5574844/,
https://academic.oup.com/ije/article/41/5/1338/709862, and the citations listed in Footnote 23.

social media, the feeling that you're "winning" often come from people "liking" or "following" you, or responding to your posts.)

Once you do decide to limit your online time, you've got three main choices:

First, you can try a **WiFi / social media blocking app**, like Forest, Freedom, or Cold Turkey. If one of these works for you, that's great. But it's easy to get sucked into procrastination before using them, and also easy to "cheat" and restore your access. (No, I'm not going to say how.)

A better solution, in my view, is to **work in a space without WiFi**. Some of the top artist residency programs, including Yaddo and MacDowell, now limit Internet access to just a library, lobby, or other common area, leaving the rest of their campus, including the artists' studios, disconnected. Similarly, you can probably find a WiFi-free library, café, or other work space where, like those pampered artists, you can work in luxurious disconnected peace and freedom. As a bonus, you'll probably find yourself working alongside some highly productive others who have also discovered the benefits of disconnecting. (Which should further boost your own productivity.)

The best solution to online distraction is to **do the bulk of your work on a computer from which you've deleted not just Internet connectivity, but (obviously) all games and other distractions**. In practice, this usually means using two computers: the disconnected one, on which you do your writing, programming, designing, and other work that requires sustained focus and concentration, and the connected one, on which you do your research, social media, gaming, etc. (In some cases, the disconnected computer can be an old one that you repurpose.) This two-computer system not only boosts your ability to concentrate, it can also help you create some empowering new options for yourself. One of my most effective productivity tricks, for instance, is this: every night before going to bed, I shut down my "connected" computer while leaving my "disconnected" one on. That way, when I return to my office the next morning, it's the disconnected one that's "alive" and beckoning me. This simple-but-powerful ritual almost always ensures that I start right in on my work in the mornings instead of getting waylaid by social media.[13]

If you do most of your work at home—or at an office, assigned library carrel, or other fixed location—working with two computers is pretty

---

[13] Productivity expert Nick Wolny came up with a similar system involving the use of two smart phones—one optimized for work and the other for personal use: see https://debugger.medium.com/how-to-use-your-old-iphone-to-set-better-work-boundaries-741f3b00fcf8.

straightforward: you leave your disconnected computer at that location, and carry around your connected one, swapping files between them using thumb drives. True, the juggling gets more complicated if you're moving around a lot and/or are working at multiple locations. (A cloud storage app can help.) Still, try to use a disconnected computer whenever possible. You could, for instance, bring your disconnected computer to the coffee shop and use your phone for urgent online activities. (And urgent calls, of course.) But keep your phone shut off and stashed away most of the time or you risk losing the whole benefit.) Then when you return home, you can boot up your connected computer and do the bulk of your online work or play.

Ultimately, you want to leave your connected computer off at all times except for those when you intentionally go online. Although it is probably harder to practice this kind of "digital minimalism," as Cal Newport calls it, in some fields than others, keep an open mind, and also keep trying out new ways to work—and play—disconnected. (See Chapter 41 for more tips on limiting your online time, and social media use in particular.)

Again, we're talking about a big divide. Some people, when I suggest that they disconnect, understand why. But others are aghast, as if I had suggested that they disconnect an arm or leg while working. A young reader of the manuscript for this book called the advice "peak Boomer," not realizing that many Boomers hate it, too. People of all ages have come to find the idea of disconnecting, even briefly, unthinkable. But ask yourself why that's so—and, also, who is benefiting from your spending long periods online engaged in low-value activities.

Especially if disconnecting seems unthinkable, that's reason enough to give it a try. Few habits have as much potential to improve your productivity and life.

6. Building Your *Sitzfleisch*

Humans are social creatures but many types of creative and intellectual work are solitary activities—and so feelings of loneliness or isolation are a common obstacle to productivity. Happily, however, all it often takes to neutralize those feelings is a "work buddy" who is doing their own project quietly alongside you as you do yours. They don't even need to be working on the same thing that you're working on: just having the company is enough to keep you going.[14]

Not all work buddies are alike, however. I learned early on that the most helpful ones tend to be those who show up right on time, or a bit early, and work steadily throughout the interval. The less helpful ones show up late and get up from their desks a time or two during the interval—each time interrupting my concentration and, I'm sure, their own. And the least helpful ones are in frequent motion, often leaving their desks.

The Germans have a handy word for the ability to sit still and stay focused on a task, *sitzfleisch*. (It translates roughly to, "having a good sitting butt.") Probably the world champion of it was the 4th century philosopher Didymus of Alexandria, who wrote 3,500 books (actually, papyrus scrolls), and whose nickname, according to historian Stephen Greenblatt in his book *The Swerve*, was "Bronze Ass." Didymus probably wasn't a fan of what we now call life balance, so you don't want to emulate him. Like all qualities,

---

[14] Good, local study buddies can be hard to find, so here's an article on apps that can pair you with remote ones: https://www.bbc.com/worklife/article/20200812-the-online-work-gyms-that-help-spur-productivity. Many people I know find https://www.focusmate.com useful.

sitzfleisch is a double-edged sword: useful for some things (e.g., getting a lot of work done), and not so much for others (e.g., staying healthy and fit).

Of course, people have different ways of learning and neurodivergence, a learning difference, a disability, and other factors can all play a role in determining how much *sitzfleisch* a person can achieve. Still, for many people, the ability to sit still and stay focused for 30, 40, or 60 minutes at a stretch is both achievable and a good thing, productivity-wise.

Whatever your current amount of *sitzfleisch* is, you can increase it by using the below **Timed Work Intervals** technique.

First, some preliminaries:

Do all your preparation before starting your work session. This includes gathering your materials, refreshing your drink, arranging the temperature (or your clothing), and using the bathroom.

Next, work **in a space without clocks**. Yeah, that includes removing the clock from your computer desktop. (I put a piece of black electrical tape over mine.) You'll stop counting the minutes, and your sense of time will, somewhat magically, simultaneously seem to both expand (so you get more done) and go more quickly (so you get less bored and impatient). You know that daydream where time stands still and so you finally have enough time to do everything you want to do? Working without a clock is probably the closest we can get to that in real life. (And yes, the technique also works for exercise and other activities where we're tempted to count the minutes.)[15]

Next, **grab a kitchen timer**—not your phone, which is distracting. (And has a clock.) Kitchen timers are cheap and come in many fun colors and styles: I highly recommend using them and other props whenever possible because doing so adds interest and variety to your work.

Now you're ready to start your Timed Work Interval:

1. **Pick a part of your project to work on.** Pick the part you most want to work on at the moment, not a part you think you should be working on. That feeling of wanting to work on something is called "inspiration," and you shouldn't waste it. (More techniques for recognizing and following your inspiration in Chapter 29.)
2. **Set the timer to count down from three minutes.** Or two minutes, or one minute, or thirty seconds: it's important to choose an interval you can easily complete.
3. **Start the timer and start working.** Work steadily but without stress or pressure. Focus on the bit of work right in front of you, ignoring,

---

[15] This "no clock" technique is also used by many stores, casinos, amusement parks, and other commercial spaces that want you to lose your sense of time so that you'll hang around longer and spend more money.

for the moment, the rest of the project, and especially any concerns or expectations you have about the outcome. (And, obviously, any outside concerns, like what's going on in one of your relationships or what you're having for lunch.)
4. If during your interval you feel yourself getting scared, stressed, distracted, judgmental, impatient, pressured, anticipatory, etc., *gently* talk yourself back to focusing on the work that's right in front of you. That fear and stress, by the way, is perfectionism—and so what you're doing here is practicing nonperfectionism while working. Cool beans!

    If you finish the bit you're working on, or find yourself getting bored or stuck, no problem. Immediately—and without fuss or drama—switch to another part of the project and keep working. (Repeat as necessary.)
5. When the timer goes off, **take a break**. (See Chapter 33.)
6. When you're ready, **repeat Steps 1–4** either with the same or a different bit of work.
7. Repeat until you're done with your work session.

After you can reliably complete three minutes (say) of stress-free nonperfectionist work, you can increase the timer to five or ten minutes. Then, 15, 20, 30, 40 minutes, etc., until you reach your desired interval length. If during an interval you accidentally glance at a clock and are disappointed at how much time is left in your interval, try reframing your situation more positively. Not, in other words, "Thirty more minutes!" *Groan.* "The time is crawling. I hate this!" But, "Wow, I still have thirty minutes left. What a gift of abundance. Okay, back to work...no rush...let's just have fun and see what I can get done."

If you ever find yourself having trouble completing your intervals, either because you're distracted or because the current project is especially difficult, don't hesitate to return to shorter ones. Remember, the important things are to: (a) finish your interval while (b) working nonperfectionistically throughout. (Eventually you'll almost certainly regain your "lost" *sitzfleisch*.)

Probably the biggest barrier to this exercise will be your Inner Perfectionist stepping in and saying something like, "Three minutes is nothing! We should go for three hours!" Feel free to ignore this misguided advice. (I'll discuss how to deal with your Inner Perfectionist in Chapter 19.)

7. The Secret to Quantity *and* Quality

I'll say it again: the goal of timed work intervals is not to get a lot of work done, or to do great work: it's to complete your interval while remaining nonperfectionist throughout. As novelist and screenwriter Steven Pressfield says of his own work sessions in his book, *The War of Art*: "How many pages have I produced? I don't care. Are they any good? I don't even think about it. All that matters is I've put in my time and hit it with all I've got."

But wait! I hear you object. I actually do want to get a lot of work done. And I also want to do great work.

Fair enough—and the secret to achieving both goals is nonperfectionism.

Let's start with **quantity**. While it may seem sensible to set an ambitious page count or other "quantity" goal, doing so creates a perfectionist overfocus on product over process. (More on this in Chapter 13.) Think about it: if quantity goals worked, wouldn't we all be super-productive by now? Most of us have been setting, and missing, such goals for years. But by setting a "process" goal of simply putting in your time while maintaining a focused but unstressed nonperfectionist mindset, you free yourself to do as much work as possible.

But don't many professionals use quantity goals? And what about my deadlines? If I don't set a quantity goal, I'll miss them all.

You're right, many professionals do set quantity goals. And you can, too—after you've overcome your perfectionism. To set such a goal while perfectionism is still holding you back, however, is only likely to backfire. (As the Pressfield quote illustrates, many professionals—including me, by the way—continue to stick with process goals.)

7. The Secret to Quantity and Quality

As for deadlines, yes, we do have a bit of a problem. We're aiming not for a quick fix, but growth; and growth takes time and can be unpredictable. For a while, your output might be lower than you'd like, or even lower than it is now. (Because you're no longer using fear and punishment as motivators.) That will be scary but stay the course and things should soon start to improve.

Now onto **quality**. In their book Art & Fear, David Bayles and Ted Orland tell a story of two groups of ceramics students, one of which was told that they would be graded based on the quality of their pots, and the other that they would be graded based on the quantity. (The more pots, the higher the grade.) I'll let them tell you what happened:

> Well, came grading time and a curious fact emerged: the works of highest quality were all produced by the group being graded for quantity. It seems that while the "quantity" group was busily churning out piles of work—and learning from their mistakes—the "quality" group had sat theorizing about perfection, and in the end had little more to show for their efforts than grandiose theories and a pile of dead clay. [Italics mine—and I'll have more to say about grandiose theories in Chapter 13.]

Quantity creates quality, in other words. Not only does aiming for quantity give you more practice, it defuses perfectionism by puncturing the illusion that you can do a perfect job. Even the most committed perfectionist is going to have to relax their standards when given just fifteen minutes to throw a pot, or five minutes to write a paragraph.

The above story also illustrates another productivity truism: you have all the talent, originality, and other creative qualities you need to succeed. This is crucial to understand because many perfectionists are convinced they don't. Always remember that we mostly use labels like "talent" and "originality" retroactively after a creative work or career turns out well. They're what philosophers call reifications: concepts that don't really exist but that we've conjured into existence by creating a word.

Of course it's true that some fields—like, say, theoretical physics and professional athletics—do have extraordinary requirements of one kind or another, but most fields don't. (And even in the "extreme" fields, hard work, good strategy, and the willingness to ask for, and accept, help will take you farther than you might think.)

As novelist Stephen King famously put it: "Talent is cheaper than table salt. What separates the talented individual from the successful one is a lot of hard work." (More on all this in Chapters 13 and 16.)

If you want to get more productive, therefore, stop focusing on your perceived personal deficits and start focusing on optimizing your work process and the context in which you're trying to work. Context includes: the types of projects you choose; your work environment; the investments, compromises, and sacrifices you're willing to make; and the mentors, colleagues, and other community you surround yourself with.

When I say that you should aim for quantity over quality, I am not suggesting that you do sloppy work. What I mean is that you shouldn't overwork your projects in a perfectionist quest to eliminate every single possible error. "Excellence doesn't require perfection," as the English novelist Henry James noted. Even in the relatively few situations where the goal truly is "zero errors," like your resume and cover letter, you achieve that not by going over your work a zillion times (which doesn't even work since we all tend to miss our own mistakes), but by working with others (e.g., a career coach and proofreader).

The above story also illustrates how even reasonable-sounding goals, such as "to do good work," are often perfectionist, reflecting an overfocus on outcomes and external recognition, shortsightedness, grandiosity, etc. These goals also can, and often do, trigger a deeply controlling (a.k.a., perfectionist) mindset where, consciously or unconsciously, you're trying to force the work in a certain direction. Creativity, however, is fundamentally a nonlinear, holistic, and liberated process: try to control it even a little and you'll shut it right down. (More on this in Chapters 25 and 29.)

The only ways to maximize your quality creative output are to:
1. Become radically nonperfectionist and use nonperfectionist work methods (see Part III) so that your ideas and inspiration can flow freely.
2. Do your time management (Part IV) to ensure that you have plenty of time not just to do your work, but to think, read, watch, listen, experience, experiment, play, etc.

One final tip for your intervals: **don't judge your experience of them.** Many perfectionists have such a strong habit of judging that, once they stop judging their work, they start judging their feelings while doing their work. "I did my work today but I didn't enjoy it," they'll grumble at me—to which I'll reply: "Fantastic! You did your work. That's the important thing. Now go out and celebrate." True: the goal is joyful productivity. But no one is joyful 100% of the time and not all projects are equally fun. (And, as I'll discuss in Chapter 31, even fun projects typically have a "yuck" stage in the middle.) Your job is to continue working while noting, but not giving too much attention to, any fears, confusions, or other obstacles that may arise. (Later you can do your obstacle-resolution work to try to defuse them.)

8. Working on the Right Stuff

Effectiveness means both doing the right stuff and doing lots—or, at least, enough—of it. In this book, I mostly focus on the "doing lots" part since what's "right" is more the domain of your teachers, supervisors, and other mentors. But here are a few general guidelines for making sure that you are, indeed, getting the most out of the time you're putting into your work.

Work with the very best teachers / coaches / editors / etc. you can. This is especially true for challenging projects like a novel or a small business startup. A great teacher can take you way beyond an average one; and beyond that, they probably also have some useful connections and other resources. Word of mouth—and especially recommendations from people with projects such as yourself—is probably the best way to find out who the best teachers are.

Another option is to join a group or association that puts you in contact with the best in your field, such as AuthorsGuild.org, GraphicArtistsGuild.org, SFWA.org (for science fiction and fantasy writers), SCBWI.org (for writers and illustrators of children's literature), and ACM.org (for programmers). These types of associations often offer a wealth of free or discounted services, including online communities and local meetups, mentorship programs, training, insurance, legal services, and assistance with networking and promotion. One caveat, though: some associations exist mainly to lobby governments and so their community offerings and benefits are scant. Others mainly exist to rake in membership fees. Only join organizations that offer a strong community and lots of member services.

8. Working on the Right Stuff

Seek out the best colleagues and collaborators. Everyone you work with should be kind, fair, great at what they do, easy to work with, and transparent in their dealings with you and others. They should also understand nonperfectionism (even if they don't use that term) and be good time managers (see Chapter 38).

Assembling the right professional community can take time but it will not only build your effectiveness and improve your outcomes, it will help make your work a joy. Just be sure to avoid anyone with a reputation for harshness or exploitation, no matter how tempting the alliance might seem in the short term. Such relationships rarely work out as well as we think they will. (See Chapter 35.)

Resource yourself as abundantly as possible. Doing so not only makes the job easier, it sends the important message to yourself and others that, "my work is important and worth investing in." To the extent that you can, invest in tools (like ergonomic furniture, see Chapter 9), supplies (like timers or those fancy colored markers you've been coveting), and services (like great teachers, etc., as discussed above) that speed your progress and make your work easier and more fun.

Learn, and use, your field's best practices. Meaning, the best ways to do the work, including how to avoid or overcome common obstacles. Many try to wing it—often, without knowing they're doing so. They take their cues mainly from superficial, hype-y media coverage, or from classmates, friends, and associates who know no more than they themselves do. Getting quality teaching or joining a good professional association, as discussed above, is the solution. (Also see Chapter 13's discussion of grandiosity.)

When asking for help, get specific. Don't hide behind generalities: tell your teacher, coach, supervisor, or mentor exactly what you're having trouble with.

Get visual. Create flow charts, diagrams, timelines, bubble maps, and other visual aids that convey the material in fresh and useful ways. (Just be careful not to overdo this so that it becomes a form of Quasiproductive Procrastination.)

Write it out. Another sure-fire way of finding out what you know and don't know.

Teach someone else. Even your dog, cat, fish, or ferret. Or, if no one's around, pretend that you're explaining the topic to a five-year-old. It's when we try teaching others that we truly understand what we know and don't know.

9. The Re-Empowerment Process I: Overcoming Your Obstacles

Creating options, as we did in Chapter 4, is a quick and easy way to re-empower yourself and it's particularly useful when you're in a rush. To get maximally productive, however, you should take the time to systematically identify and resolve all your obstacles to doing your work. I discuss the first part of this process, obstacle identification, in this chapter, and the second part, obstacle resolution, in the next.

Obstacles fall into six general categories:

- **Project-Related.** Your project is difficult, confusing, boring (see Chapter 32), overwhelming, etc. Or your teammates aren't doing their job. Or there's a mismatch between you and the project—or, even, between you and your job or career. Maybe you lack the right skills or preparation for it. Or maybe you really want to be doing something else.
- **Organization-Related.** The project or job is being done for an employer but you're not given the supervision, training, authority, money, space, or other resources to succeed. An incredibly common problem—and the blame is almost always put on the employee rather than the people responsible for ensuring the employee's success.
- **Resource-Related.** Your workspace (whether provided by you or an employer) is uncomfortable, inconvenient, noisy, or ill-equipped. Or you lack a well-functioning computer or other necessary piece of equipment.
- **Time-Related.** You don't have enough time. (Part V will help.)

- **Personal Issues.** You have physical or mental health challenges or a learning difference.[16] Or you're dealing with perfectionism or one of the other barriers to productivity I discuss in this book. Or you're dealing with serious relationship, financial, and/or other problems. (Or are worried about someone else who is.)
- **Societal Issues.** You're distracted by events in your community or the larger world. (And perhaps also anxious, depressed, or grief-stricken about them.)

A word about that "Resource-Related" category: it's more important than it might seem because **a lot of procrastination begins in the body**. (You feel a bit uncomfortable, and that feeling builds until you have to get up from your chair.) There's also a safety issue because a bad setup can cause an injury. (Once, after working on a too-high desk for just a few weeks, I got an elbow injury that took two years to heal.) So, always use a comfortable and adjustable ergonomic setup.[17]

In ergonomics, seemingly little things can make a big difference. I'm a big fan of adjustable book stands, which are cheap and make reading (especially big textbooks or reference books) far easier on your neck and shoulders. If you're doing a lot of typing I really recommend using a "wavy" keyboard that lets you hold your wrists at a natural angle. (Try one in a store for just a moment and I think you'll be sold.) Footrests are also cheap—or free, if you create yours from a cardboard box. (Top it off with a spare pillow or bit of foam for extra comfort.)

There are lots of sources for cheap but high quality office furniture, including Ikea and Craigslist. And don't forget lighting: adjustable, variable-setting desk lamps are also cheap.

I know many people don't have a lot of money, but to the extent you have it, investing in furniture and supplies that make working easier, safer, and pleasanter is an excellent choice. It also sends the crucial message to both yourself and others that, "This work is important, and I'm committed to it. And my health and safety are also important."

---

[16] As per the "On Using the Correct Toolset" note at the beginning of this book, if you're dealing with a physical or mental health issue, or a learning difference, please consult a specialist.

[17] Here are two good, quick ergonomics primers: https://youtu.be/i1wIcVRP9xQ and https://youtu.be/9mJDs2CGZRI. And for a deep dive: https://ergo.human.cornell.edu/ergoguide.html.

Returning to the entire list, that's a lot of potential obstacles. Picture each as a string, and all of those strings snarled up in a giant ball; then, picture that giant snarly ball blocking—as in writer's block or creative block, get it?—the "path" you're trying to walk along. (Meaning, the plan or schedule you're trying to follow for the day.) Some people visualize their block as a boulder or wall, but I think a snarl is a much more useful representation because it reflects the fact that your block is actually made up of multiple smaller "strands" (obstacles) that you can "untangle" (resolve) one at a time. Even better, the more untangling you do, the easier the rest of the snarl becomes to deal with.

The next time you feel tempted to procrastinate, therefore, don't waste time with negative self-talk. Instead, just grab your computer or notebook and make a list of all the obstacles that are blocking your ability to do your work. Be sure to include any "small" ones, such as that your chair is uncomfortable and your lighting poor. The small ones do add up—and, like icebergs, are often bigger than they seem.

Table I shows a sample Obstacle List for a grant-writing project.

Table I: Sample Obstacle List for a Grant Writing Project

Category	Obstacles
Project-Related	1. I've got a whole bunch of pieces and don't know how to put them together (a.k.a., confusion or overwhelm). 2. No matter how great the proposal is, I doubt this project is going to get funded (a.k.a., futility). 3. I actually don't even know how to write parts of the proposal. What they're asking for is confusing.
Organization-Related	4. A coworker was supposed to have sent me some statistics I need but hasn't done so yet. 5. I disagree with the approach that we're proposing for the work but my supervisor shuts me down whenever I try to bring that up. 6. Even if this project does somehow magically get funded, I have no idea how we're actually going to do it. It's not really in our remit and I don't think we have the resources. 7. Will our main contract even be renewed for next year? I may be writing a grant for a project that no one will be around to fulfill.

9. The Re-Empowerment Process I: Overcoming Your Obstacles

Resource-Related	8. My computer keeps freezing. 9. I have to constantly stop to unjam the printer. 10. It's hard to concentrate in this space with fifteen other people working around me.
Time-Related	11. My supervisor assigned me this grant proposal on top of all my usual work. I'm swamped! 12. I have another big deadline this week. 13. People keep interrupting me.
Personal Issues	14. I'm exhausted. I never get enough sleep. 15. I think my antidepressant prescription needs to be adjusted. It's not working as well as it used to. 16. My brother is going through a hard time and I'm really worried about him. 17. I am constantly worried about money. I don't make enough and my college loans eat up so much of it. (And what if we don't get our main contract renewed? I might be out of a job.)
Societal Issues	18. The current political situation really upsets me and makes it hard to concentrate.

Eighteen obstacles may sound like a lot but it really isn't: most people come in at anywhere between fifteen and forty. (Yes, forty.) In fact, many people are shocked at the number of obstacles they come up with because much of the time we're often only half-aware of many of our obstacles...

...which is why you should do Exercise 3!

Exercise 3

Make an Obstacle List for a project you've been procrastinating on. After you've finished, take a moment to reflect on it, and especially to feel some compassion and respect for yourself. Maybe at times you've bashed yourself for your supposed laziness or lack of discipline. (Or others have.) Now it turns out you've actually been struggling honorably to do your work in the face of many obstacles.

Note: What's even better than doing an Obstacle List to help you identify your barriers while working? Doing one before you get started so that you can identify potential barriers and nip them in the bud. Get in the habit of doing such a pre-emptive list, especially before your big or important projects.

Obstacle Resolution

After you've created your Obstacle List, start listing possible solutions to each obstacle and then implement the best solutions. Table II shows the beginning of our grant writer's solutions list.

Table II: Sample Solutions List

Category	Obstacle	Possible Solutions
Project-Related	I've got a whole bunch of pieces and don't know how to put them together (a.k.a., confusion or overwhelm).	1. Use journaling to clarify exactly what the problems are. 2. Ask someone for help. (Your supervisor is the obvious choice; but perhaps you also have other coworkers, colleagues, and mentors you can ask.) 3. Make a to-do list; tackle one item at a time. 4. Use the solutions in Parts II and III of this book to help defuse perfectionism.
	No matter how great the proposal is, I doubt this project is going to get funded (a.k.a., futility).	1. Journal for clarity: is there a specific reason you feel this way and can it be addressed? 2. Ask yourself if you are being fatalistic or otherwise perfectionist. 3. Discuss the situation with your supervisor, a grants officer, or a mentor. 4. If, after doing the above, you're pretty sure that the proposal won't, in fact, be funded, that would be an argument for writing the shortest and quickest "acceptable" proposal. So, ask yourself and others what you can omit.

9. The Re-Empowerment Process I: Overcoming Your Obstacles

	I actually don't even know how to write parts of the proposal. What they're asking for is confusing.	1.	Consult your supervisor or your organization's grants office.
		2.	Can you access previous proposals that were funded? They might give you a clue as to what the funder is after. (Sometimes you'll find these online and sometimes the funding agency will provide them on request.)

I'm aware that most of the solutions listed above aren't rocket science—and that's kind of the point. Once we stop panicking and start problem solving, the solutions can be startlingly obvious.

Also, note how most of them involve asking someone else for help. I'll be talking more about that in the next chapter.

In any case, two very cool things happen when you start coming up with solutions:

1. **You empower yourself.** Every problem-solving step you take—from identifying the problem to journaling about it, discussing it with others, listing possible solutions, trying out a solution, improving that solution, and implementing the improved solution—empowers you some, thus making it easier for you to take the next step. It's a virtuous cycle! (The opposite of a vicious cycle.) And the more empowered problem-solving you do, the more empowered, in general, you become.

2. **You become less afraid and more optimistic.** That's partly because of the empowerment and partly because the solutions often turn out to be easier than we expect. You write, "ask someone for help," for instance, and immediately think of someone you can ask. Or, "get more sleep," and immediately think of some evening events you can cancel so you can do that. However, even with the solutions that take more work, or even years of work (e.g., learning to cope with a chronic physical or mental health condition), and even for the problems that will never be fully solvable (e.g., a difficult family situation), or are largely out of your control (e.g., the societal problems), you're still way better off problem-solving than procrastinating.

Some of your solutions, especially for problems in the Personal category, may involve seeing a therapist. This is yet another area where it pays to "invest in the best." (I speak from experience, by the way.) If cash is limited, find one who offers a sliding scale fee structure.

Your therapist should not only offer services congruent with your needs—trauma work, eating disorder work, relationship counseling, addiction recovery, etc.—but feel like a good fit in terms of personality and communication style. And after the first couple of getting-to-know-each-other sessions, your work together should start yielding meaningful change in your life. If your first therapist isn't doing all this for you, keep looking until you find one who does.

Exercise 4

Come up with solutions for the obstacles you listed in Exercise 3 and start implementing the best ones.

10. The Re-Empowerment Process II. Why You Need to Ask for Help Early and Often

Got a problem?

Well, someone you know probably has a solution.

Oh, I know: you don't like to ask for help. You're afraid you'll look dumb—although asking for help is the opposite of that. Or you don't want to impose on anyone. Or you think it's somehow more admirable to go it alone. Sure: try that, for a little while, anyway. But if you really need help—and why wouldn't you? We all do.—it's best not to be in denial about that, because: (a) as discussed in Chapter 2, the desire to go it alone, no matter how well-rationalized, is often rooted in deeper issues; and (b) a failure to ask can lead to some spectacularly time-wasting forms of Quasiproductive Procrastination (QP), such as:

- Trying to figure out which direction to take your project when a mentor can tell you in a flash.
- Struggling endlessly with a computer problem when the friendly gurus at the local computer fix-it center, or your organization's information technology department, know exactly how to fix it.
- Wasting time, and risking failure, doing a difficult project from scratch when a more-experienced person can tell you what works and doesn't work. (Otherwise known as "reinventing the wheel.")
- Having both halves of a conversation in your head when you really should be talking to the other person. (An incredibly common form of QP.)

The bottom line is that isolation, no matter how tempting or well-rationalized, is not your friend—and asking for help is really one of the most empowering things you can do. The latter is probably why, often, after someone emails me for help, I'll get a second email from them a few minutes later saying, "Never mind—I figured it out for myself."

You'll also be further empowered, of course, by the actual help you wind up receiving, as well as by your strengthened relationship with your helper. (Who will themselves be further empowered by having helped.) So many great outcomes just from the simple act of asking for help! And so, **you should ask for help early and often**. Ask when potential problems are still small so you can nip them in the bud. Or, ask even before they arise so you can avoid them entirely. (Example: "I'm planning to do X. Can you tell me the best way to do it? Also, what problems do people typically encounter, and how can I avoid those?") Do this not just for your work, but all your important endeavors.

Let me say it again: isolation, no matter how tempting or well-rationalized, isn't your friend.

11. The Best Solution to Procrastination

The best solution to procrastination is, obviously, to not need to do it in the first place—and you can achieve this, at least mostly. To see how, let's take a closer look at our friend the Disempowerment Cascade. Turns out, it's an interaction among three internal personae (or "voices"). They are:

The Fragile Creator. The persona who's trying to work. They're fragile not because you're weak but because the work is challenging and you're facing many obstacles.

The Terrified and Terrorizing Perfectionist. (Also sometimes known as the Inner Critic or Inner Bully.) This persona is both hypercritical and terrified of failure, which isn't a great combination. They're also almost certainly suffering from some other problems that I'll be discussing in Part II, including shortsightedness, negativity, and a fixation on supposed personal flaws. They are, in fact, the persona responsible for Chapter 3's disempowering monologue: "What's wrong with you?," "Why are you so lazy?," etc. And when the pain they cause becomes intolerable, the third persona is invoked...

The Rebellious Procrastinator. Contrary to what you might guess, they are *not* your enemy. Their job is to rescue the fragile Creator from the bullying Perfectionist, and in some ways they represent the best part of you: the part that is willing to fight for freedom, authenticity, and self-expression, and against bullying, coercion, and injustice. The problem is that they are invoked in circumstances of panic and stress, and are therefore disempowered and not great at problem solving. In fact, the only "solutions" they can come up with to address the problem of the perfectionist bullying are:

1. *Rebellion.* As in, "Why am I stuck inside doing this stupid work when everyone else is outside having a great time? It's not fair. Screw it, I'm

going out!" (Recall Timothy Pychyl's point, from Chapter 2, about how procrastination often originates as a rebellion against authoritarian parenting.)
2. *Helplessness.* As in, "I can't even try to get started on my work."

Here's the tricky part: although your Inner Procrastinator can only come up with those two bad solutions, they can come up with infinite ways to "sell" them to you. So if it's not, "It's nice out and dammit I deserve a break," it's "I should do all these less-important tasks first so that tomorrow I can focus better on my big project." Or, "A little TV won't hurt."

Always remember that **the fundamental goal of productivity work is to be able to show up on time and do what you had planned to do.** Maybe not every single time—we all have emergencies and "off" days. But most of the time. When you accept that foundational truth and stay mindful of it while you work, you will become less susceptible to your Inner Procrastinator's manipulations.

Of course, the best solution would be to retire your Inner Perfectionist persona, because it's in response to them, and as a protection from them, that you invoke your Inner Procrastinator in the first place. I'll discuss ways to do that in Part II.

Part II

Compassion

12. Perfectionist Myths and Realities

Note: The first quarter (roughly) of this section (Chapters 12–15) provides an overview of perfectionist attitudes and behaviors. After that, I'll discuss solutions (Chapters 16–23). And I'll end (Chapter 24) with a discussion of ambivalence, which is closely linked to perfectionism. Also, just to remind you: in this section and elsewhere in the book, I do some labeling, dichotomizing, and generalizing to keep the prose concise. So you'll see a lot of "Perfectionists do this…" and "Nonperfectionists do that…" In real life, however, I would avoid doing that. (It's okay to label a behavior, but not a person—and anyhow, no one is entirely perfectionist or nonperfectionist.)

Perfectionism is a set of attitudes and behaviors that make it hard, or even impossible, to do your work. Unfortunately, there's a lot of confusion out there, with many people confusing perfectionism with "having high standards" or "caring about my work," and some even thinking, "It's good to be a little perfectionist." That can make it hard to even identify the problem, much less solve it.

Let's be crystal clear: **perfectionism is *never* a good thing.** It *never* helps and *always* hinders your creativity and productivity. It can also hinder you in other areas of your life, including your relationships and health. After you've finished this section, I hope you will commit to rejecting perfectionism in all its forms, and in all areas of your life. I especially hope you'll reject it at times you feel you've failed or had a setback. At such times, the temptation to revert to guilt, shame, deprivation, and other perfectionist punishments will be strong. But you need to be stronger. (More on that in Chapter 22.)

Kayla's story, below, shows us how perfectionism can create serious problems for a writer—but also how, with the right help, that writer can overcome their perfectionism and resolve those problems.

Kayla didn't just want to write a novel—she needed to write one. She had, over the past decade, published several short stories and essays, some in prestigious journals. But in her heart of hearts, she felt that you weren't a real writer until you had written a book.

Also, she hoped that publishing a well-respected novel would finally put to rest the comments from family and friends that, "maybe it was time to settle down and do something more practical."

The only trouble was that she was having trouble writing. It wasn't just that her novel was her first long work, and thus intimidating. It was also that it was autobiographical, and Kayla was determined to create as true and nuanced a portrait of her family's complicated history as she could, including both the positives (the close family ties, hard work, and perseverance) and negatives (poverty, addiction, and loss). She was finding it hard to balance all those elements, however—and she also constantly worried about how her family would react when they saw the book. Would they see her as "airing dirty laundry" or worse, holding them all out for public judgment? There had already been grumblings about some of her earlier autobiographical pieces.

Kayla felt trapped, in other words, between telling the story she wanted to tell and the knowledge that doing so was likely to upset those she loved.

And that wasn't her only source of pressure around her writing. An agent she had met at a literary conference had pronounced her work-in-progress "timely," and invited her to send him the manuscript when it was done. Kayla, with perhaps a bit too much optimism and eagerness to please, assured him she'd have it ready soon. Now, months later, it was still only half done—and she was terrified she was blowing her big chance.

Kayla was also distracted by an awful incident that had happened at that same conference. She had signed up for a workshop with a writer whom she had always admired—in fact, the chance to have him critique her work was the main reason she had decided to attend in the first place. But then, right in the middle of the workshop, and in front of all the participants, he had harshly criticized one of her chapters, calling it "clichéd" and "derivative." Kayla still cringed to recall the episode—and now, whenever she tried to write, she was constantly on the alert lest her work showed any sign of those flaws.

12. Perfectionist Myths and Realities

Kayla knew she should be setting her concerns aside while writing but was having trouble doing so. Her worries kept crowding into her thoughts and crowding out the story she was trying to tell. She now also spent most of her time revising chapters she had already written—and revising them again, and again, and again—instead of moving onto others.

Nor did it help that, whenever she wrote a scene, she wasn't happy with the result. Her prose seemed banal, especially when compared with that of her idols.

This was all incredibly frustrating—especially as it seemed, sometimes, as if everyone and their cousin were not only out there writing novels but getting them published. One of her friends was having a great time writing a couple of romance novels a year and making good money from them. It wasn't the kind of writing Kayla herself wanted to do but she couldn't help envying her friend's productivity and financial success.

Eventually, it got to the point where Kayla had trouble even approaching her computer. In desperation she contacted a former teacher whom she knew to be both compassionate and savvy about the creative process. The teacher—let's call them "Muse"—agreed to do some freelance coaching for their former student at a reasonable hourly rate.

During their first meeting, Muse listened patiently while Kayla laid out nearly all her worries and concerns. (Omitting only the episode with the harsh workshop leader, which was still too painful to share.) This was the first time Kayla had voiced them all, and she was surprised at how much better she felt simply from having done so.

Muse listened carefully, then explained the various ways perfectionism was blocking her ability to write. They then showed her techniques for defusing it (Chapters 18-24), and others that would support and encourage her creativity (Part III).

Back at home, Kayla tried the techniques and, sure enough, her productivity improved.

Muse also encouraged Kayla to email the agent and tell him that she was still working on the book and still interested in showing him the manuscript when it was done, "but at this point it looks like that will probably be next year." Kayla worried that he'd see her as "flaky" and "unserious"—and also that, if she delayed, she'd run out the clock on "timely" (whatever the agent had meant by that)—but knew she had no choice. Fortunately, the agent had the courtesy to respond quickly, although his response—"looking forward to it"—was worryingly on the terse side. Muse, however, encouraged Kayla not to dwell on it. "People are busy," Muse said. "But it's a good sign that he got back to you. And, by the way, even if this falls through, you'll almost certainly have more 'big chances.' In any case, let's just focus on the writing itself for a while, versus where you hope the book lands."

At their second meeting, Kayla summoned the courage to tell Muse what the workshop leader had done. When she finished, Muse shook their head angrily, noting that, "People like that have no business teaching." She urged Kayla to: (a) do her best to forget the harsh instructor's comments (and perhaps, along with some other workshop participants, write to the conference organizers suggesting they not hire him again), and (b) join, or create, a critique group that would give her more useful feedback.

As Muse spoke, Kayla felt her shame easing—and then, afterwards, was able to write even more easily.

At their third meeting, Muse addressed Kayla's concerns of offending her family. Muse said that that was a very common concern among writers of autobiographical fiction and nonfiction, and that there were no easy answers. They advised Kayla to, "write the story you want to write and that wants to be written. Later on, you can decide how and when to publish it, and if you want to use a pseudonym." She also encouraged Kayla to identify some trusted family members who could advocate for her work to the rest, but also to recognize that, "some people will never get what you're doing and that's their right—but maybe don't give them too much power."

Kayla realized, with relief, that she had more options for dealing with her family than she had thought.

With all this great help, Kayla was able to regroup and get more relaxed about her writing—and the words, pages, and chapters started to flow.

13. How Perfectionists Think

In this chapter, I discuss the most common perfectionist attitudes; and in the next, I discuss some common perfectionist behaviors. Obviously, there's a lot of overlap between attitudes and behaviors, with the attitudes often causing the behaviors. (And vice versa, by the way: our behaviors also help form our attitudes.) But the attitudes discussed in this chapter can cause many different types of antiproductive behaviors and so it's useful to discuss them separately.

(1) **Perfectionists devalue process and overvalue product/outcome**. For them, it's all about getting the A, getting published, getting the promotion, or having some other kind of notable success. Nothing else matters, including how hard they worked, what they actually accomplished (in terms of learning, performance, etc.), what internal or external barriers they overcame, and any intelligence, courage, kindness, integrity, or other admirable qualities they may have displayed along the way. This viewpoint isn't just fundamentally unfair and inhumane, it creates vast pressure and sucks all the joy out of your work.

Also, reducing the actual work you're doing to a mere means to an end makes it hard to stay motivated on big projects in particular.

Overfocusing on outcomes is actually dangerous because you're never guaranteed a good one. You could be really well prepared for a job interview, for instance, and still do disappointingly because it was poorly conducted or happened to focus on your weakest area. (Or, you were sick or distracted by personal problems.) Or, you could ace the interview and still not get the job because of nepotism, discrimination, or (more benignly) a budget cut. True: most of the time your outcomes should be commensurate with your efforts. If they're not, something's wrong, and you should consult your mentors. It's also okay to hope for a good outcome so long as you don't get too attached to that hope. But, for the most part, you want to avoid having any strongly held expectations.

(2) **Perfectionists define success narrowly and often unrealistically.** To them, only an A—or, better yet, A+— is acceptable.

Your supervisor comments that your report was "very good"? Big deal! If it wasn't "excellent" or "outstanding" you've failed.

You're a runner-up in a tough arts, athletic, business, or other competition? Who cares? You didn't win.

Obviously, this attitude also creates vast pressure. **It also redefines your successes as failures, which is one of the most demotivating, demoralizing, self-sabotaging, and pointless things you can do.** (As already noted, the perfectionist tendency to confuse "success" and "failure" is why I frequently put those words in quotation marks.) See Chapter 21 for more on the difference between realistic and unrealistic definitions of "success," and Chapters 22 and 23 for more on "failure" and "success."

(3) **Perfectionists are grandiose.** Grandiosity is when you think the normal rules of productivity don't apply to you, or—put somewhat differently—that things that are difficult or even impossible for others should be easy for you. This can lead to:

- Unrealistic goal setting. ("Even though I'm already incredibly busy, I should be able to take on this additional huge project.")
- Underestimating the difficulty of challenges. ("This will be a piece of cake!")
- Unwillingness to research and plan ("Boring!") or ask for help. ("I'll figure it out myself.")
- Expecting yourself to succeed despite being under-resourced. ("Last year it took five people and $800 to do this community project, but we should be able to do it this year with only three people and $400.")
- Tendency to think you or your project are special or even unique. ("My project is so cutting-edge that there's no one I can turn to for help.")
- Lack of respect for experience and expertise. ("I know my supervisor / coach / mentor wants me to do the project this way, but I'm going to do it that other way because it's faster.")
- Silly pointless rebellions. ("I won't bother getting a haircut for my job interview because my resume says it all.")
- Stinting on self-care. ("I only need four hours of sleep a night." Or "I don't need to see a therapist for my depression.")

13. How Perfectionists Think

- Trivialization of your pain or suffering. ("Who cares if I'm unhappy? It's my work that matters.")

Grandiosity can also cause you to take on **overly ambitious projects**. The underlying problems here are often insecurity and a desire to impress others. I can usually tell if someone's fallen into this trap because: (a) the project in question is too huge a leap from their previous work, (b) they lack the training and/or preparation to do it, (c) they're overfocused on externals (e.g., creating a fancy explanatory slideshow)[18] versus the nuts and bolts of the work, (d) they're overfocused on others' anticipated glorious reactions to their work, (e) they're isolated (no mentors, collaborators, etc.), and/or (f) their plan has an overintellectualized or overcomplicated quality. (Out of all of those, I would say that (e), the lack of mentors, is the biggest red flag.) Don't get me wrong: ambition is great. But taking on an overly ambitious project is, like all perfectionism, a dead end. Overly ambitious projects tend to bog down in Quasiproductive Procrastination (QP) because the person won't let the project go, but also has no real idea of how to proceed—and so, they wind up burying themselves in pointless, and often repetitive, busy work. Then, when they can no longer maintain even the illusion that they're making progress, the QP usually devolves into full-blown Unproductive Procrastination (UP), at which point it's only a matter of time before they abandon the project.

Sometimes, of course, projects just mushroom out of control. That's actually a good problem to have, because what it's really indicating is that you're inspired. But it's still a problem you need to solve. (Again, talk with your teacher / supervisor / coach / mentor, etc.)

Perfectionists usually have a compelling-sounding (to them, at least) rationalization for their grandiose ideas. Point out, for instance, that a perfectionist is overscheduling themselves and they'll reply that they are "efficient" or "well-organized." Or, point out that they need to plan their big project, and they'll reply that they're "good at winging it." But the rationales fall apart at the slightest scrutiny. No one, no matter how well-organized, can cram ten hours of work into five hours—and while you may be able to wing a small or unimportant project, winging a big or important one is a recipe for disaster.

(4) **Perfectionists overidentify with their work.** As discussed in Chapter 3.

---

[18] Or, as discussed 5, focusing on how your retail business looks, versus the financial "guts" of its operation.

(5) **Perfectionists are shortsighted.** They live in one big, hyper-judgmental "now," in which not just every project (or task) is of utmost importance, but every moment of every project. **Moment by moment, many perfectionists are constantly comparing their work and progress to an idealized vision of how they think they should be performing**. This means that they are constantly judging themselves as falling short and constantly berating themselves for that. (More on comparisons in the next chapter.)

It's a pretty miserable way to live.

Shortsightedness doesn't just result in a highly pressured and miserable work experience, it's also **one of the main reasons perfectionists quit projects.** (And jobs, careers, art, activism, etc.) Whenever a perfectionist hits a "bump" in their project—even a small and/or ordinary one—they can't see their way past it and get so discouraged that they quit. Obviously, pathologizing will also contribute to this predicament, and so will the disempowered belief that you have fewer options than you really do.

And how does a perfectionist quit a project? Often, by glomming onto a shiny new one that they hope will be, "the one that finally keeps me interested enough to finish." But it never is, for the simple reason that the problem isn't the projects, it's the perfectionism. (And if you're thinking that some people do the same thing with romantic relationships—perpetually ending them when they get challenging and moving onto others that they hope will magically go better—yeah, you're right.)

(6) **Perfectionists are impatient**. Because of their overfocus on product, overidentification, and shortsightedness, they need—no, crave—their success *now*. This impatience doesn't just make for a miserable work process, it compromises the quality of your work (Chapter 26) and also impairs your ability to learn and grow. (Because learning and growth both take time.)

Perfectionists are also impatient in their careers, craving youthful success. Many see life as a kind of race, and are constantly comparing their progress to that of their friends, acquaintances, siblings, and others, including celebrities. Gail Godwin captured this attitude brilliantly in her short story, "Mr. Bedford and the Muses":

> [My novel] was beginning to assume more urgency than before, since I had subtracted Reynolds Price's birth date from the date of publication of his first novel. (Ian, the new boarder, had actually

seen me doing this arithmetic in the flyleaf of the book...he surprised me by saying, "I used to do that, too." "Don't you anymore?" I asked. "Not once they all started being younger.")

(Note, also, the comparisons.)

The ubiquitous "30 Successful People Under 30"-type articles not only feed this impatience, they also have another big problem, which is that they heavily favor the privileged. As podcaster Kristen Meinzer puts it: "What would happen if [those types of articles] excluded people whose parents paid for their college education and/or business startup, paid the down payment on their first place, or paid the bills while they worked unpaid or low-wage internships?"[19] (More on competition in the next chapter.)

(7) **Perfectionists are negative.** As noted in Chapter 4, they habitually underestimate and devalue their available options and outcomes. Even worse, they devalue their accomplishments, others' accomplishments, and others' willingness and ability to help them. They also mentally filter out positive results and outcomes, seeing only their "mistakes" and "failures." Tell a perfectionist you think their work is excellent except for one tiny thing and they'll only hear the tiny thing—and probably inflate it into a Great Big Thing.

This negativity can lead to an even more disempowering **scarcity mentality** in which you think that you either "aren't enough" (not smart, disciplined, creative, talented, or attractive enough, etc.) or "don't have enough" (money, time, help, ideas, etc.) to succeed. (See, also, Chapter 14's discussion of fixations, and note how this scarcity mentality aligns with the idea of not having enough good options or potential outcomes.)

A scarcity mentality can also manifest itself in the belief that it is somehow nobler or more impressive to succeed in the absence of adequate resources. Examples range from the centuries-old "starving artist in the garret" stereotype to the more recent "I ate ramen for five years before my big break" media profiles of successful artists and entrepreneurs. Please note that what I'm objecting to here is not scarcity itself—scarcity is neither a virtue nor a vice, just an unfortunate circumstance that many people must deal with—but a romanticizing of scarcity. It's vital that you not buy into this romanticizing because, perfectionist myths aside, it is very hard—and, often, impossible—to succeed when you're under-resourced.

(8) **Perfectionists distrust success and often reframe their successes as failures.** If a perfectionist gets a good outcome, they'll come up with five reasons the achievement should be dismissed, or should have been

---

[19] https://twitter.com/kristenmeinzer/status/1281287686662377476

better. (E.g., "the project was easy" or "my opponent was having an off day.") And if their work is going easily, they'll worry that they're not challenging themselves enough. They might even add some unnecessary work to it just to make it harder!

Sometimes there's a cultural component to this problem. You might have been taught, for instance, that humility is a virtue and talking about your successes, even to yourself, is boasting. There's a difference, however, between taking pride in your achievements and boasting about them. Pride is based on an objective and humane assessment of yourself and your work. It's an emotion that you primarily communicate to yourself, although others can certainly sense and respond to it. It is also incredibly motivating, so you don't want to cheat yourself of it.

Boasting, in contrast, is usually grounded in insecurity, and primarily aimed at others. (Who aren't fooled.) I'll be discussing it some more in the next chapter.

Remember that the word "humble" derives from the same Latin root as "humus," meaning earth or ground. The classical virtue of humility isn't about being self-effacing or overly modest: it's about being grounded.

Perfectionists can also suffer from **impostor syndrome**. It can take several forms, including the belief that you haven't earned your success or are somehow fooling everyone with it, and the belief that you really don't belong in the professional or other communities you wish to be a part of. Those from marginalized or under-represented communities can be especially vulnerable, as can those who have experienced harsh criticism or rejection. (See Part IV.) Regardless of the cause, dealing with your perfectionism can help alleviate the problem.

(9) **Perfectionists are rigid**. This shows up, especially, in a tendency to stick with a solution long after it's clear it's not working. If a perfectionist keeps getting distracted by their noisy environment while they're trying to work, for example, they'll "keep trying till I can concentrate, dammit!" More than once, a writer has justified this particular form of rigidity to me by pointing out that Jane Austen supposedly wrote her novels in her parlor, surrounded by her boisterous nieces and nephews. To which I reply: (a) so what? And (b) comparisons are perfectionist—as I discuss in the next chapter. (I also happen to think that the emphasis that many place on this particular narrative is actually kind of sexist, supporting the idea that a woman should subordinate her life and work to others' needs.)

Or, if they're in a difficult relationship, they'll keep using the same ineffective coping strategies over and over again.

13. How Perfectionists Think

Recall, from Chapter 3, that productive people are problem-solvers who, when they encounter a barrier to their productivity, deal with it as quickly and decisively as possible.

I've saved the worst for last:

(10) **Perfectionists try to use punishment as a motivator.** It usually takes the form of either a shaming label (e.g., "I'm such a loser for not doing well."), a threat ("If I don't do well, then I'm really going to be in trouble."), or deprivation (e.g., "I'm going to sit here until I get it right. No breaks!"). What's confusing is that these tactics sometime seem to work in the short term. But **punishment always leaves you more fearful and disempowered around your work and, thus, less able to do it in the future.** (Which is why I say perfectionists "try to" use it as a motivator.) Also, we become habituated to punishment, so it eventually stops working even in the short term. The first time we call ourselves, or someone else calls us, "lazy," for example, it feels terrible and might actually shame us into doing our work. But the fifth or tenth time? Yawn.

Because perfectionists are constantly feeling like they failed, they are also constantly punishing themselves—which, needless to say, is a terrible way to live. Punishment is also alienating and provokes opposition. That's easy to spot when the "punished person" and "punisher" are different people—think of a teenager rebelling against their domineering parents. But it also happens within us when we respond to our bullying Inner Perfectionist by calling up our rebellious Inner Procrastinator. (As discussed in Chapter 11.)

The biggest problem with punishment, however, has nothing to do with whether it works: it's that it's inhumane and immoral. You should never do it to yourself or anyone else.

Those are the main perfectionist attitudes. See how they can all work together to create a trap? Overfocus on outcomes, and define success narrowly and grandiosely, and you're pretty much guaranteed to "fail," especially if you're both impatient for your success and mistrustful of any successes you do achieve. Overidentify with that "failure," and you'll feel even worse, especially if you can't shortsightedly see past it. And respond to all that by punishing yourself, and you're guaranteed to feel not just miserable, but hopeless—especially if you rigidly refuse to consider any other way of approaching your work.

And procrastination will start to make sense as an escape from all that pain and hopelessness.

14. How Perfectionists Behave

Below are some common perfectionist behaviors, all of which derive from one or more of the attitudes discussed in Chapter 13.

(1) **Labeling**. By now, I hope you understand why you shouldn't use punishing/shaming labels like "lazy" or "undisciplined." But even positive labels can be problematic. Being labeled as "gifted" or "talented" can put a lot of pressure on you, leading to perfectionism and procrastination.

Some people get into trouble by overidentifying with a professional label such as "artist" or "engineer." It's okay to use those labels, only don't do so in a way that increases the pressure on yourself or limits your options. Beliefs such as, "an artist should be willing to sacrifice everything for their art" and "an engineer should only be concerned with facts and never feelings" are both incorrect and unhelpful. (Also notice both statements' grandiosity.)

Be careful even with more objective labels. You might think of yourself as "pragmatic," or "idealistic," or "caring," for instance. That's wonderful—until you take things too far and your pragmatism becomes stodginess, your idealism becomes shallow fantasy, and your caring becomes overgiving (Chapter 45). As it turns out, many of our vices are simply our cherished virtues taken just a bit too far.

You also want to avoid labeling your work. A professor once told a friend of mine that her paper was "brilliant": she spent the rest of the semester terrified of not living up to that high standard. Perfectionists also often label their projects as "hard" or "easy," then dichotomize those labels so that "hard" becomes, in their mind, impossible, and "easy" trivial. This leads to a lot of fear (in anticipation of your supposedly hard stuff) and discouragement (when your supposedly easy stuff turns out to be harder than anticipated). Better to let those labels go and let your work just be your work. And when praising someone else's work, it's a good idea to follow psychologist Carol Dweck's advice from her book *Mindset*, and praise not their outcome or what you consider to be their intrinsic talents (e.g., intelligence), but their "growth-oriented *process*—what they accomplished through practice, work, persistence, and good strategies." (Italics mine.)

The worst labels tend to be **hyperbolic**. Statements like, "my novel is garbage," "my workout is hell," and, "I'm the worst girlfriend ever" do nothing but increase your fear and disempowerment around the activity in question. And while we're on the topic of word choice, **be aware that there are a few seemingly benign words that, all by themselves, are enough to make a statement or thought perfectionist**. One is "**just**," as in the statement, "I just have to read [or write] ten pages." The implication—and dangerous expectation—is that your work should go quickly and easily. Ditto for "**only**," which is often used the same way. Meanwhile, "**finally**" often reflects a perfectionist impatience, as in this sentence: "I finally got my work done." And last but not least, we have "**should**," as in, "I should be able to handle a difficult job with long hours and also be able to be there 100% for my family." I actually love this example because it's so common and also so incredibly grandiose: the speaker is literally saying that they should be able to be in two places at once. And that "100%" is the perfectionist cherry on the ice-cream sundae: we're human, not programmable robots, and none of us can be there "100%" for anything. (And even robots have their down times.)

In my productivity classes, we often do an exercise entitled "Perfectionism Test," where students identify the perfectionist elements in a group of sentences. After we're done, I say, "There's one more perfectionist thing on the page—can you find it?" Most students can't. "It's the title!" I point out. "Why call this a 'test?' Why not call it an 'exercise' or even a 'game?'" The simple act of swapping in "exercise" for "test" allows everyone in the room, including me, to relax.

These kinds of perfectionist word traps are everywhere. So please watch your words and keep things as light and playful as possible.

(2) **Comparisons.** Perfectionists constantly compare themselves to anyone and everyone, including family members, friends, strangers, and famous people both living and dead. They'll compare themselves on personal qualities like talent, discipline, and tenacity, and also on any element of personal or professional success. Perfectionists will even compare themselves to *themselves* at a higher level of performance. A perfectionist who was once able to write a great short story or essay over a single weekend, run a four-

and-a-half-minute mile, or perform a faultless Brahms piano sonata will spend years or decades expecting to repeat that exceptional achievement, all the while bashing themselves for failing.

Speaking of Brahms, he was, relentlessly and from a young age, compared with Beethoven, to the point where people would joke that his First Symphony would actually be "Beethoven's 10th." And you know what? It took him 21 years to produce that symphony. The miracle was that he was able to produce it at all, given the enormous pressure and public scrutiny he labored under. "You can't have any idea what it's like always to hear such a giant marching behind you," he bemoaned in a letter to a friend.

Many perfectionists also constantly compare themselves to—and constantly bash themselves for falling short of—an idealized version of an identity or role that's important to them, such as the "dedicated activist [or artist]" or "dutiful child of immigrant parents." Philosophers call this the "Nirvana Fallacy," and it is an especially demoralizing and exhausting habit. Many perfectionists also constantly compare their work sessions to an ideal and constantly bash themselves for supposedly falling short in terms of quantity or quality. They'll even compare themselves to some mythical creator for whom the work is always easy and joyful—and then bash themselves for falling short of that ideal as well.

Comparisons can obviously be a useful analytical tool. A perfectionist comparison rarely is, however, because the goal of a perfectionist comparison isn't objective analysis, but to shame yourself into doing better. One sign that your comparison is perfectionist is that it leaves you feeling bad; another is that it omits crucial information. A perfectionist poet, for instance, might bash themselves because their poems aren't as good as those of their favorite Famous Poet, ignoring the crucial points that: (a) the poems they admire are likely to be the Famous Poet's best, (b) Famous Poet likely developed their craft over decades, and (c) even the most brilliant poets have written their share of clunkers. Oh, and also that: (d) fame is often the result of luck (including fortuitous timing) as well as, or even more than, talent.

All of the above, of course, applies to the stars in any field.

Finally, our poet might also bemoan the fact that they are making less money in their editorial job than a friend is making in finance, omitting the crucial points that they love their work and would hate finance.

Whenever you feel bad about yourself or your work, there's usually a perfectionist comparison involved.

(3) **Competitiveness** often goes hand in hand with comparisons. Sure, competition can be fun and help you excel. But perfectionists often focus just on winning, and they'll also try to compete in situations that aren't, or

shouldn't be, competitive. That gratuitous competition is a drag in real life—no one enjoys being around the person who always has to win. But it's even worse, in some ways, on social media. Many platforms explicitly or implicitly encourage constant comparisons, either with your friends or, worse, with the carefully curated and photo-edited feeds of celebrities and influencers. Psychologist Melissa G. Hunt, whose research on the mental health harms of social media I cited in Chapter 5, says that these constant "social comparisons" are among social media's worst aspects.

Perfectionists also often forget that, in an unfair world, even many fair-seeming comparisons and competitions really aren't. Many people, for instance, compare their progress against that of others with generational wealth, family connections, and other advantages that they don't have. (Recall Kristen Meinzer's quote about the "30 Under 30" articles, from Chapter 13.)

(4) **Boasting and Misplaced Pride.** Perhaps because they're embarrassed about their underproductivity, like poor Eric was in Chapter 1, perfectionists often feel the need to boast about how hard they're working or the massive sacrifices they're making. "Yeah, I probably shouldn't have pulled three all-nighters last week," they'll say, sounding rueful and abashed. But you can hear the pride underneath.

Boasting is tedious and rude, and it doesn't fool anyone.

Perfectionists also like to boast about how tough their work is. Examples: "[Name of field]: only the strong survive," and "[Name of field]: we separate the wheat from the chaff." Along with also being tedious and rude, this kind of boasting can discourage those from under-represented groups, or who haven't had the privilege of an elite education, from participating.[20] Similarly: "[Name of field] can't be taught—you've either got the talent or you haven't." Along with also being tedious, rude, and wildly exclusionary, this kind of boast is also a form of victim-blaming that also, and probably not so coincidentally, absolves bad teachers and others from having to take responsibility for their professional lapses. (Also, note the dichotomizing.)

(5) **Hoarding.** As noted earlier, perfectionists hoard their work. Unfortunately, the more you do that, the more scared and disempowered around your work you become and the more you need to do it. (It's a vicious cycle, in other words.) Another way to visualize this is that hoarding creates a wall between you (and your work) and those with whom you should be interacting, including not just your supervisor, editor, agent, gallery owner,

---

[20] https://www.nytimes.com/2020/11/16/science/weed-out-classes-stem.html

or whoever else is waiting to receive your work, but also potential collaborators, mentors, and audiences. To be clear, you're not just keeping your work behind the wall, but advice, support, and opportunities outside of it. And the more you hoard, the bigger, taller, and more impenetrable that wall gets. (Solutions to hoarding in Chapter 32.)

(6) **Fixating.** Perfectionists are generally self-critical, but they also often have one or two areas where they are especially self-critical. I call these "fixations," and they often start when someone harshly or publicly criticizes you or your work, and that criticism then becomes a part of your self-image that you struggle with. Especially if the critic is someone you respect (Chapter 34), the criticism—be it, "Dialogue isn't your strong point," or "You're an impractical dreamer," or something else—soaks right in and becomes something you dwell on. An even worse variation of this is when someone expresses a bigoted viewpoint—e.g., "women can't do math"—and that becomes part of your self-image. That's called "internalized oppression," and I also discuss it in Chapter 34.

As with many of the problems I discuss, it's often the most caring and dedicated people who fall prey to fixations because their caring makes them vulnerable.

Of course, our society and media are themselves hugely fixated on certain things, including wealth, looks, and popularity (including social media popularity), so it's easy to get fixated on those even if no one directs a criticism specifically at you. Additionally, as discussed in Chapter 7, society also fixates on glamorous intangibles like "talent" and "originality," and so it's easy to get personally fixated on those as well, especially if you're in a creative field.

Again, notice how all the perfectionist behaviors can reinforce each other, so that, for instance, labeling and comparisons can cause a fixation, which in turn can cause hoarding—which you might then try to cover up, or compensate for, via boasting. And notice how exhausting it all is. Constantly struggling against perfectionism will wear you out until you have no energy or enthusiasm left for your work or anything else.

Exercise 5

Expand Exercise 3's (Chapter 9) Obstacle List using the perfectionist characteristics I've discussed in Chapters 13 and 14. If you're overfocusing on outcomes, narrowly defining success, overidentifying with the work, etc., describe the effect that that behavior is having on your productivity, and on your overall health and happiness.

Exercise 6

1. List all the perfectionist attitudes and behaviors you see in Kayla's story (Chapter 12) and discuss how each might be blocking her ability to do her work.[21]
2. List all the perfectionist attitudes and behaviors you see in Eric's story (Chapter 1), and discuss how each might have blocked his ability to get his degree.

---

[21] Some answers (you might find more): overidentification ("needed to write" a novel), using her project as a source of legitimacy or validation (justify her career choice), labeling ("real writer," "literary," "flaky," "big chance"), narrow definition of success / trying to control the outcome (wants to create, "as true and nuanced a portrait" of her family as she could ," "well respected"); overfocus on product and external recognition (the workshop leader, her family, and mythical reviewers); grandiosity (perhaps too complex a story for her first novel?); comparisons (to writers she admired), fixations (persistent worries about her writing being clichéd or derivative). Whew!

15. Where We Learn Perfectionism

The perfectionist attitudes and behaviors discussed in the previous chapters all have one thing in common: they go against accepted best practices for productivity, learning, and growth. So where do we get the idea that they're useful? From the media, to start with. Perfectionist narratives tend to be simple and compelling, and so the media loves them. That's why you constantly see:

- Stories of "spectacular," "easy," "overnight," "solo," and "against-all-odds" success in the arts, business, sports, romance, etc.
- Stories that gloss over the process a person used to succeed, focusing instead on the glorious outcome.
- Stories that glamorize or exalt poverty, deprivation, and suffering. (For instance, depictions of "starving artists" who don't seem to mind their poverty.)
- Stories that exalt punishment, suffering, or "tough love."
- Stories where the characters live in what I call "magical affluence"— e.g., the barista or freelance writer who somehow manages to afford a fabulous New York City apartment. These households also always seem to magically clean and stock themselves, which is also perfectionist.
- Stories where the person supposedly has the high-paying job needed to support the fancy lifestyle but you never actually see them doing that job. (In the real world, high-paying jobs tend to dominate your life.)
- Stories that trivialize the realities of human existence and relationships. If you've read *Atlas Shrugged*, for instance, you may recall how,

at the end of the book, Ayn Rand's capitalist heroes all wind up living together in effortless peace and harmony despite their many economic and romantic conflicts. Come on! Have you ever seen that happen in real life? (For the record, Rand's own personal relationships were, to put it mildly, a mess.[22])

A lot of **advertising** is also perfectionist. Many ads overfocus on product at the expense of process ("Just do it!"), grandiosely trivialize human suffering ("No pain, no gain."), depict narrow and unrealistic outcomes ("Use this mascara and you'll look like a supermodel."), use flawed comparisons ("before and after"), promise quick solutions to difficult problems ("Lose 10 pounds in two weeks!"), and trivialize human relationships ("Drink this booze and you'll be sexy and popular.").

The Parents' Trap

Perfectionism is so pervasive that even many parents, teachers, coaches, and other mentors have internalized it. See if you can identify the perfectionist characteristics in these common parental statements:
1. "How come you only got a B?"
2. "It's easy!" (When you're struggling with something.)
3. "Why can't you do as well as your brother?"
4. "Get over it!" (When you're hurting from a painful rejection.)
5. "Sarah is great at science and Adam is great at art."[23]

Make no mistake: it's often the most dedicated and caring parents who fall prey to this kind of perfectionism. But it can still hurt, as this real-life episode illustrates:

> A while back, a friend got a call that her 12-year-old daughter had broken her wrist during soccer practice and was on her way to the emergency room with her father, who had been coaching. My friend hurried to meet them there, but when she arrived, she unexpectedly found a daughter who wasn't just injured, but irate. Apparently, at some point during the drive, Dad had told Daughter,

---

[22] See Barbara Brandon's biography, *The Passion of Ayn Rand*.
[23] Some answers (you may find more): (1) narrow definition of success; (2) overfocus on product / trivializing of process; (3) comparison; (4) grandiosity (you shouldn't feel pain); (5) comparison.

in response to her crying, to "stop being a wimp." Talk about *literally* adding insult to injury! Small wonder, then, that Daughter's first words to her mom weren't, "Ow, my wrist really hurts!" but an outraged and accusatory, "He called me a wimp!" The emotional and moral pain of being perfectionistically labeled had completely trumped her actual physical pain.

Dad, meanwhile, just stood there looking guilty and confused. What had he done wrong? He hadn't meant to cause his daughter additional pain, of course. But he, too, had grown up surrounded by perfectionism and had internalized many of its messages.

Sometimes, during discussions of perfectionist parenting, someone pushes back on the whole "don't pressure or punish your kids" idea, saying something like, "My parents pushed [or punished] me, and *I* turned out okay." Of course, we have no idea, in such cases, what kinds of pushing and punishments actually took place, or how the person's life might have differed had they not been subject to them. Perhaps the pushing and punishments were relatively mild and occurred in a context of authoritative parenting (with lots of rules but also lots of affection), rather than authoritarian parenting (lots of rules but little affection), as discussed in Chapter 2. Or, perhaps they had an exceptionally kind teacher, coach, or other mentor whose influence helped to neutralize the perfectionism and other harshness.

Or perhaps they were resilient for another reason.

No matter. As discussed in Chapter 13, it doesn't matter whether punishment "works," or seems to. It's an inhumane practice that you should take an ethical stand against, both for yourself and others.

Situational Perfectionism

People often ask me whether someone can be "born perfectionist." It's a good question. Every parent knows that kids are born with different temperaments, and that some definitely do have a tendency to be critical and/or judgmental. Such kids, if they're lucky enough to receive compassionate parenting, can usually avoid the trap of perfectionism. Unfortunately, what most of us get, in a perfectionist society, is perfectionist parenting, and so, even if we weren't born with an especially critical temperament, we still wind up falling into the trap. (And, obviously, those who were born with a critical temperament are at risk for having that tendency reinforced.)

Many events can also trigger what I call **situational perfectionism**, which is when an event or circumstance causes your perfectionism to spike. These include:

- A transition, like those discussed in Chapter 2.
- A perceived failure or rejection (Chapter 22 and Part IV) that makes you more afraid of possible future failures.
- A perceived success (Chapter 23), if it causes you to feel more visible and scrutinized. An example of this would be the writers, like Ralph Ellison and Harper Lee, who, after having had a notable success with their first book, either failed to produce a second or took decades to do so. (A phenomenon so prevalent it's got a name: "the second book problem.")
- An opportunity you're afraid of squandering. For instance: "Now that I've got this great new job [or new computer, or paid coaching, or some other advantage], I'd better do amazing work!" Or, during vacations: "I've got two whole weeks off; I'd better make the most of them!" (Either in the sense of having fun or getting ahead of your work.) Or, for parents, at the start of the school year: "Now that the kids are back in school, I should really be able to get some stuff done."
- A need to justify others' efforts or sacrifices on your behalf. ("My partner is super supportive, so the least I can do is be super productive." Or, "my parents sacrificed a lot for me, so I'd better be a success.")
- Being someone from an under-represented group, especially if your situation causes you to feel extra-scrutinized, or that your "success" or "failure" reflects on your group.

If you're subject to any form of situational perfectionism, that's just one more hurdle you'll need to overcome in your quest for joyful productivity. Remember: **there's nothing wrong with wanting to do great work. The problem is when you cross the line into perfectionism and your work becomes painful, stressful, or deprivational.**

Exercise 7

Take another look at the situation you examined for Exercise 3 and see if you can find some situational triggers that caused your perfectionism to spike.

> **Note:** We've finished our discussion of the nature and origins of perfectionism. Time to move on to the solutions.

16. Nonperfectionist Attitudes and Behaviors

Nonperfectionists hold the opposite of the attitudes, and do the opposite of the behaviors, described in the previous chapters. Specifically, they:

(1) **Focus on the process of doing their work**, as opposed to the desired outcome. A process focus not only takes a lot of the pressure off, it helps you connect with the work's intrinsic pleasures—and that, in turn, helps you stay motivated. As Steven Pressfield puts it in *The War of Art*, "The professional has learned that success, like happiness, comes as a by-product of work. The professional concentrates on the work and allows rewards to come or not come, whatever they like."

(2) **Define success broadly and holistically**. Yes, nonperfectionists want that great outcome. But mostly they measure success based on whether or not they've done their best—meaning, whether they've worked steadily and with good focus. After that, it's whether they've accomplished some good learning or growth, with both interpreted broadly. (Often, as per Chapter 28's discussion of trial and error, the valuable lesson is a greater understanding of what *doesn't* work.) Other important accomplishments might be: staying cool under pressure, treating others well under difficult circumstances, overcoming (even partially) a personal or institutional barrier, connecting with a new mentor or collaborator, and having enjoyed the work.

Another example of a broadly defined success is when someone joins a sports team not just, or primarily, to compete, but for the health, recreational, teamwork, camaraderie, coaching, and other benefits of participation. (Ditto for someone who joins a musical, artistic, or other group for similar benefits.)

16. Nonperfectionist Attitudes and Behaviors

(3) **Stay grounded.** Nonperfectionists know that grandiosity is delusional. (It's actually a gambler's mentality and linked to low self-esteem.[24]) So, they try to err on the side of humility and do *extra* planning, get *extra* help, etc. They also choose their projects out of a sincere interest rather than a need to impress. And they take their time management (Part V) seriously: never, for instance, trying to pack ten hours of work into an eight-hour workday.

(4) **Maintain a healthy emotional distance from their work.** Nonperfectionists know that even their "important" work is merely something they do, and not a justification for their existence or a window into their innermost soul. They also know that obstacles are a normal part of any project, and not a reflection on them personally; and so, when they encounter one, they don't pathologize. They also know that everyone is better at some things than others, so they don't expect themselves to be exceptional in every area. (Or in any area: the whole idea of being "exceptional" is fraught.)

(5) **Take the long / broad / high view.** Nonperfectionists understand that there's a point in pretty much every big project—and, sometimes, more than one—where you feel stuck and hopeless. (See Chapter 31's discussions of the Anti-Honeymoon and Vast Middle.) Also, that a lot of problems that seem serious at the time turn out not to be (Chapter 22). And that all projects, including the biggest and most important-seeming, are mere "station stops" along the journey of their life and career.

These and other long-range perspectives help them to stay grounded and motivated, even in the face of setbacks.

(6) **Are patient.** Nonperfectionists understand that it takes time to do quality work—and, often, way more time than we anticipate. (More on this in Chapter 26.) They also understand that, perfectionist fixations on youthful success aside, most successful careers are built gradually over time. And they understand that when they rush their work or other activities, they not only compromise their chances of success, but cheat themselves out of potential joy and fulfillment. (More on the evils of rushing in Chapter 39.) So, they strive to remain patient and to work systematically and with deliberation, even when the pressure's on.

(7) **Are positive.** Nonperfectionists work to stay objective—or, even better, a bit positive. Positivity (a.k.a., optimism) is often disparaged as naive or childish, but it is a fantastic basis not just for joyful productivity, but a happy life.[25] Sure, it's a form of expectation, so you don't want to overdo it.

---

[24] https://pubmed.ncbi.nlm.nih.gov/29455443/
[25] Also a healthier and longer one:
https://www.nytimes.com/2020/01/27/well/mind/optimism-health-longevity.html.

But a little too much positivity is way better than negativity, and way, way better than cynicism (which is when you expect the worst from everyone and everything around you). Not only are negativity and cynicism profoundly disempowering, they repel others, and so can damage your professional and personal relationships.

(8) **Abundance mentality.** Nonperfectionists also have an abundance mentality that encourages them to not only fully utilize all available resources, but persevere in finding new ones. **They explicitly or implicitly grasp, in other words, a key foundation of productivity work: that you are enough, and have enough, to succeed.** Enough talent, originality, and other personal qualities, for one thing (as discussed in Chapter 7); and also enough time, help, and other resources. Just to be clear: this doesn't mean that you have every single quality or resource you want, or could use. Probably no one has that. But enough, at least, to get you mostly where you want to go. (Important note: I'm not denying that many people don't actually have enough money, time, or other resources, due to either their personal circumstances, systemic inequalities, or both. The specific problem I'm addressing here is the many people who do actually have enough but don't think they do.)

(9) **Own their successes.** Nonperfectionists are comfortable owning and celebrating (Chapter 23) their successes. If anything, they take some extra pride and satisfaction from them—always taking care, however, to avoid the trap of overidentification—since it never hurts to err a bit on the side of nonperfectionism. This is an area where hanging out with the right crowd can really make a difference. Be among people who are comfortable owning their successes and it will become easier for you to own yours.

Nonperfectionists also don't waste time questioning whether they are challenging themselves enough. If they're in doubt, they ask a mentor.

Nonperfectionists also know that it's perfectly okay—and a wise strategy, actually—to take on the occasional easy project. They also know it's fine to benefit from the occasional lucky break.

(10) **Reject impostor syndrome.** Nonperfectionists recognize that impostor syndrome is a story we tell ourselves that has the power to harm us, and therefore do their best to reject that narrative. If actual incidents of exclusion have contributed to the problem, they work to heal from those, perhaps with the help of counseling. (Again, this is an area where hanging out with the right people can really help.)

(11) **Are flexible.** If a solution isn't working, nonperfectionists don't sit there and try to make it work: they quickly try another. They also always have a "Plan B," just in case.

16. Nonperfectionist Attitudes and Behaviors

(12) **Never punish themselves.** Unfortunately, even after you intellectually and ethically reject punishment, it can still be a hard habit to break. (Chapter 20 offers some suggestions for dealing with that.)

Relatedly, nonperfectionists also understand that **there is no cheating in antiperfectionism work.** I don't mean that you shouldn't cheat: I mean that you literally can't cheat. The moment you overfocus even a little on product, or put even a little pressure on yourself, or try even a little to control your outcome (Chapter 28), you're back in the realm of perfectionism.

(13) **Resist labeling and hyperbole.** Whenever possible, nonperfectionists use precise and nuanced descriptions, such as: "I've got ten pages to read tonight" or "I need to learn to follow through on my commitments better." This precision may sound boring in comparison to perfectionist labeling and hyperbole, but at least you aren't disempowering yourself via your language.

(14) **Avoid comparisons.** Nonperfectionists are comfortable evaluating their achievements on their own merits, without constant comparisons. While they may look to more successful people as role models and inspirations, they avoid strong or over-direct comparisons, especially if they don't know the whole story behind the other person's success. Especially, they are careful to not get sucked into comparisons on social media.

Nonperfectionists also avoid **envy**, which accomplishes nothing except for making the envious person miserable. (It's the only one of the so-called Seven Deadly Sins that is no fun.) Nor do they dwell on their former successes, except to: (a) appreciate them, and (b) try to replicate the conditions that made them possible.

(15) **Avoid excessive competitiveness.** When nonperfectionists compete, their goal is not to triumph over others, but to do the best they can while, as much as possible, enjoying and otherwise benefiting from the experience. (If they win, that's just the icing on the cake.)

Ultimately, nonperfectionists understand that creative and intellectual endeavors are fundamentally individual journeys of discovery—as is life itself. (More on this in Chapter 25.) While it is possible, and essential, to learn from others, in the end, we each need to chart our own course. As the novelist Bernard Malamud put it, "Eventually everyone learns his or her own best way. The real mystery to crack is you."

The creative journey is fascinating and important. But a habit of relentlessly comparing yourself to, and competing against, others can undermine it.

(16) **Don't boast or indulge in misplaced pride.** If they feel the need to do so, they take that as a sign that something's wrong. (Boasting is often a sign of insecurity.)

(17) **Share their work early and often.** Nonperfectionists know that, in contrast to the "walls" that hoarding builds between you and others (Chapter 14), sharing creates "bridges." They also understand that the more, and earlier, you share, the more bridges you create, and the easier it becomes to keep sharing, both with your current project and future ones. So, they share early and often. Early on in a project, for instance, a nonperfectionist might share their idea and plan with a mentor and get feedback on those. Then, as they progress, they'll share bits and pieces of their actual work. Sometimes they'll do this in the context of asking a question. ("Here's what I've done so far; what do you think?" Or, "I'm not so sure about my conclusion, is it okay?") And sometimes they'll share just for the heck of it, because they know that sharing is empowering. ("Hey, I dig this thing I just wrote, just wanted to show it to you, no reply needed.") (Obviously, the more casual forms of sharing are best done among friends.)

(18) **Hand their work in on time.** Nonperfectionists don't give themselves permission to routinely miss deadlines. A great technique for achieving this, by the way, is to give yourself an early deadline that occurs somewhat sooner than your real one. Tell yourself often enough that your deadline is Wednesday, for instance, and you'll eventually start to believe it—and then it will come as a pleasant surprise when you realize that it actually is Friday, and so you have a couple of extra days to finish. (Of course, sometimes we miss a deadline due to an extenuating factor, like an illness or family crisis. That's a different situation from what I'm discussing here, which is a habit of missing deadlines even when there is no extenuating circumstance.)

After they've handed in their work, nonperfectionists **(19) don't sit around waiting for the outcome** (whether they got the award or grant, whether their paper was accepted by a journal, etc.), but move right on to the next project. This not only helps them get more done, it also helps them to not overreact when the outcome, be it "positive" or "negative," finally does arrive.

(20) **Work to overcome their fixations, and to avoid developing new ones.** Nonperfectionists use journaling and, if necessary, counseling to help overcome their fixations. They might even take a media literacy class to help them better understand media manipulations and machinations. And

16. Nonperfectionist Attitudes and Behaviors

they are also careful to filter their media and other inputs to limit their exposure to unhelpful and sabotaging messages. (See Chapter 37 for more on using social media safely and effectively.)

So that's our list of nonperfectionist attitudes and behaviors. Do nonperfectionists do all of these things 100% of the time? Of course not: they have their slip-ups like everyone else. (And that "100%?" Perfectionist!) The important thing is that, when they do make a mistake, they skip the self-reproach and focus on learning from the experience and making a plan to do better next time.

I'll share the techniques nonperfectionists use to overcome their perfectionism starting in Chapter 18. But first, we need to discuss the three most critical things every nonperfectionist knows.

Exercise 8

Is there an activity you love but aren't perfectionist about? (Sometimes called a hobby.) Maybe you love to cook, even if your meals aren't gourmet quality. Or knit, just for fun. Or swim, even if you're not on a team. Maybe you've even had a "disaster"—like a meal where everything went wrong, or a scarf where you dropped a whole bunch of stitches—and been able to laugh it off. That's some excellent nonperfectionism right there. See if you can bring that same playful and process-focused approach to your work and other "serious" endeavors.

If you don't have such a hobby, I urge you to develop one, as the benefits will be many. Perhaps there's an activity you've always wanted to try but haven't yet. If so, go for it!

17. The Three Most Important Things Nonperfectionists Know

The three most important things nonperfectionist people know are:

(1) **All perfectionist narratives are lies.** Poke any perfectionist statement and all kinds of inconvenient truths come flying out: the "overnight success" turns out to have worked for years prior to their breakthrough; the "young" or "solo" success was helped by family money and connections; the "natural beauty" required days of preparation before the photo shoot, plus photo-editing afterwards; and the "glamorously" broke artist or activist didn't actually enjoy being broke (and their work suffered).

Nonperfectionists also know that social media is a horror-show of comparisons, competitiveness, and pretty much every other perfectionist characteristic we've been discussing. And so, they use it judiciously and are selective about who they hang out with. (More tips on how to safely use social media in Chapter 37.)

All this brings us to the second important thing nonperfectionists know, that...

(2) **Perfectionism never helps and always makes things worse.** As mentioned before, perfectionism is inhumane and unethical, so should be avoided for those reasons above all.[26] But it doesn't even work! Think about

---

[26] There's a growing literature on the deleterious effects of perfectionism on teenagers and young adults, especially. See, for example:
https://www.nytimes.com/2019/02/20/health/teenage-depression-statistics.html,
https://www.cbsnews.com/news/a-lost-girls-diary-alexandra-valoras/, and
https://www.theatlantic.com/magazine/archive/2015/12/the-silicon-valley-suicides/413140. If you're having suicidal thoughts please call the National Suicide

17. The Three Most Important Things Nonperfectionists Know

it: we're all swimming in a societal ocean of perfectionism, and many people bash themselves perfectionistically every day, hoping that that will somehow magically lead to increased productivity. If perfectionism really worked, wouldn't we all be super-achievers? But of course we're not.

As mentioned in Chapter 13, it's confusing that perfectionism sometimes seems to work in the short-term (but always leaves us more fearful and disempowered around our work). **The truth is that we succeed despite our perfectionism, not because of it, and so, one of the very worst perfectionist lies is that you need to suffer to succeed.** (More on this in Chapter 20.) Especially resist the myth of the "tortured" artist or activist, for reasons of not just productivity, but your health.[27]

So yes: dream big. Work hard. Make your commitments, investments, and sacrifices. But don't work in the absence of a sound strategy that's been reviewed by knowledgeable mentors. And don't work past the point of health, happiness, and a balanced life. Or, put another way: always strive to act out of love, not fear.

All of which brings us to the most important thing nonperfectionists know:

(3) **"Never go there."** Never succumb to the urge to do the things I discussed in Chapters 13 and 14. Now, that's easy enough to do when your work is going well. But we all have times when we're underproductive or otherwise think we've "failed," and when that happens, the temptation to revert to pressure and punishments can be strong. But you need to be stronger. The key is understanding, not just intellectually, but deep in your bones, that perfectionism never helps and always makes things worse.

This may all sound philosophical, but it is deeply practical. By refusing to give in to the temptation to be perfectionist, nonperfectionists not only keep themselves healthy and safe, but ensure that they are able to get back on track with their work as soon as possible.

"Never go there" is a very strong instruction, but strength is exactly what's needed. **Procrastination and perfectionism are strong and sneaky habits that are often fed by denial and self-deceit: you won't get far trying to counter them with weak, wishy-washy measures.** You

---

Prevention hotline at 1-800-273-8255 (TALK). And here's a list of global anti-suicide resources: https://www.speakingofsuicide.com/resources.
[27] See, for instance: https://www.minnpost.com/second-opinion/2016/02/tortured-artist-meme-lacks-good-evidence-says-british-psychologist/ and
https://www.independent.co.uk/voices/world-mental-health-day-tortured-artist-dangerous-myth-pain-art-depression-suicide-a8576971.html.

need to confront them with strength, certitude, fortitude, and the conviction that, "I never pressure or punish myself or anyone else."

18. The Nonperfectionist Mindset: Introducing Your Inner Compassionate Adult

Nonperfectionism is a collection of attitudes and behaviors that support your ability to do your work. Unfortunately, just as there are myths around perfectionism, there are also myths around nonperfectionism. Many people confuse it with "having low standards," "being self-indulgent," or "not being accountable for my mistakes." Not so! It's about doing your best and holding yourself accountable but not crossing the line into unethical and counterproductive punishments.

Remember the three personae from Chapter 11's Disempowerment Cascade: the Fragile Creator, Terrified/Terrorizing Perfectionist, and Rebellious Procrastinator? Someone's missing, and that's the Compassionate Adult. That's the persona who not only understands and respects your ambitions, but actually knows how to do the work, and is an expert at recognizing and overcoming obstacles.

They are the persona who should be leading the others.

The core work of overcoming perfectionism, therefore, is developing your Inner Compassionate Adult persona and voice. Below are two techniques for doing that. They're relatively simple, but don't let that fool you: they are powerfully transformational.

Reframing to Compassion

The first is a **reframing** technique: you catch yourself thinking perfectionistically—often after some kind of mistake or "failure"—and GENTLY interrupt that train of thought and reroute to nonperfectionism.

Instead of thinking: "I did badly on that project. I'm stupid."

You think: "Well, I'm disappointed in the outcome. But it was a hard project and I didn't have all the resources and support I needed. Even so, I know I should have started earlier, and worked more consistently, and also reached out more often for help. Well, I won't waste time feeling bad or calling myself names. Instead, I'll just make a plan to do better next time."

Instead of thinking: "I can't believe I didn't get that job. I'm such a failure."

You think: "I knew I should have practiced more for that interview. Well, I'm pretty disappointed, but will try to get past that. I'll apply for some other jobs this week, and be sure to practice more before future interviews. Also, I'll show my resume and cover letter to my mentors and see if they have any suggestions for improving them."

Instead of thinking: "I can't believe I dropped my phone and broke the screen. What a klutz!"

You think: "Well, that sucks! But getting upset won't 'unbreak' it and, besides, everyone drops stuff. But yeah: in the future, I'll definitely be more careful when taking my phone out of my bag."

Notice how the nonperfectionist statements are longer than the perfectionist ones. That's because, in contrast to reductive perfectionism, nonperfectionism aims for a more nuanced and accurate view. Notice also how, even though the nonperfectionist statements skip the guilt, shame, blame, and other punishments, they still maintain accountability. Nonperfectionism isn't about giving yourself a pass (a perfectionist's worst fear). Rather, nonperfectionists know that you don't have to punish yourself to learn and grow.

The best way to approach this reframing is to focus on one perfectionist characteristic at a time; then, when you've mostly succeeded in reframing it—so that you skip the self-shaming and go right to nonperfectionism—work on another. Don't, in other words, try to fix "everything, all at once," because that's...well, I think you know what that is! Expect gradual improvement and also some lapses and backsliding, which you should always respond to with patience and compassion. (Remember that the whole point of the work is to grow the voice of your Inner Compassionate Adult.) Give yourself lots of affirmation for your successes while ignoring any "failures," except to learn from them.

A good way to locate your nonperfectionist voice is to ask yourself, "What would I tell someone else in this situation?" That works because we're often more compassionate with others than with ourselves. Treating ourselves worse than we treat others is a common mistake and a

18. The Nonperfectionist Mindset: Introducing Your Inner Compassionate Adult

grandiose perfectionist might actually feel some pride about doing that. But it's as misguided as every other perfectionist behavior. We need to be at least as compassionate with ourselves as with others.

Some have described the nonperfectionist voice as that of the "good grandparent" or "wise teacher" or "benevolent coach." These adult designations are no accident: nonperfectionism is an empowered mature viewpoint. Your Inner Creator, Inner Perfectionist, and Inner Procrastinator are all fearful, and thus at least somewhat psychologically regressed—because fear causes us to lose capacity—which is why they keep coming up with the same ineffective solutions. Once you introduce an Inner Compassionate Adult into the mix and let them lead, however, your Inner Perfectionist will start to relax, as frightened children do when a competent adult steps up. Then your Inner Procrastinator will see that they are no longer needed and gracefully exit the scene.

Leaving your Inner Creator free to do their job!

If the idea of reframing your thinking (or your inner monologue, see below) sounds silly or shallow, remember that perfectionism itself is a learned behavior that harms you every day. So why not work to replace it with something better? When you do, you should see a boost not just in your productivity, but your mood. In fact, the more reluctant you are to do this reframing, the more you probably need to do it.

I sometimes tell people that they shouldn't "indulge" in perfectionist thinking. What I mean by that is that, despite all the pro-perfectionist societal conditioning out there, perfectionism is ultimately a choice you make, and so is nonperfectionism. Yes, change can be weird, as I'll discuss in Chapter 20. But commit with all your heart to overcoming perfectionism and a new and better world can open up to you.

Developing a Nonperfectionist Inner Monologue

It's great to interrupt a perfectionist self-criticism and replace it with something more self-affirming. But it's even better not to have that self-criticism to start with. Replacing your perfectionist inner monologue with a nonperfectionist one will strengthen your nonperfectionism and make it less likely that you'll succumb to perfectionism during times of trouble.

Perfectionists, as discussed earlier, live with a more-or-less constant sense of failure that is fed by a more-or-less continuous self-critical inner monologue: "What's wrong with you? Why are you so lazy?" etc. You need to replace that monologue with a nonperfectionist, self-affirming one like this:

"Okay, let's get started...Good work starting on time...Okay, that sentence has got a few problems, but I can fix those later...And hey! That's a really great point I just made! Let's have some fun expanding it..... Okay, that part doesn't really work but let's just leave it in there for now. Got plenty of time to fix it later...This is turning into a really interesting project. I'm so glad I chose it..."

This kind of monologue helps build your confidence and enthusiasm—and, again, please note that you are not abandoning your critical judgment and accountability. You still see the problems with your work and are committed to fixing them: you're just not panicking or shaming yourself over them.

Pay particular attention to your monologue at the beginnings of work sessions because that's when your fears tend to be at their highest. If your monologue, at that fragile moment, is all about how, "My work is a chore...How tedious...I'd rather be partying...Why me?...This sucks...etc.," of course you're going to have trouble starting. Instead, monologue in an affirming way that also helps you reconnect with the interesting ideas or problems that brought you to the project to start with. For example: "Okay! Time to work on my report. I'm really looking forward to delving into those numbers. I think our team did some good work over the past few months and I'm really looking forward to revisiting and sharing those results. I also think there are some areas where we could have done better, and where I'd like us to do better in the future, and so perhaps this analysis will help with that." This kind of inner monologue, especially when combined with the nonperfectionist work habits I describe in Part III, can mean the difference between wanting to avoid your work and actually being impatient to start. So, try it. Please note that, in many cases, it's worth taking the time to actually write out your monologue, both because the act of writing can yield clarity and strength, and also because what you write can often transition seamlessly into your actual work. Go ahead and set your timer for a Timed Work Interval (Chapter 6), and go for it.

The above techniques will help you develop a nonperfectionist mindset that will make it easier for you to do your work at just about any time. One word of caution, though: try not to rush or put pressure on yourself while learning to use them because that's perfectionist. Yup, I'm telling you not to be perfectionist in your quest for nonperfectionism. (It happens.) **You'll know you're doing your nonperfectionism right when you're able to sit down and do your work when you had planned to do it, and for as long as you had planned to do it, with a minimum of stress, fuss, hesitation, etc.** Also, because you start getting more ideas for your work even

18. The Nonperfectionist Mindset: Introducing Your Inner Compassionate Adult

when you're away from your desk. (Because you're not perfectionistically self-censoring.) There you'll be, minding your own business on the bus or at the grocery store, when wham! You get a good one! Please, please, please: take notes. (Either on paper or using your phone's voice recorder—whatever works for you.) What productive people know is that there aren't just a few good ideas out there, but lots of them. You just gotta: (a) be nonperfectionist and (b) take notes.

But what about when perfectionism strikes hard during a work session and you're tempted to procrastinate? The next chapter tells you how to deal with that.

Exercise 9. Intentionally Erroneous Emails

Here's a sweet little exercise that packs a nonperfectionist punch. All you have to do is send out some emails or texts with intentional errors in them. Those errors could be anything from aN typo, to a mispeling, to some wEiRd formatting, to any kind of random STR*&^qq(ANGENESS.

That's it! "What's the catch?" I hear you ask. The "catch" is this: perfectionists hate this exercise. They hate making errors and the idea of making one intentionally is simply inconceivable (as Vizzini would say). Yet, what's the harm? (So long as you're sending them out to friends and not, say, the chair of the scholarship committee.) This exercise is useful in both helping you to see just how perfectionist you are, and in helping you to loosen up a bit and build your nonperfectionism.

I've seen people try to cheat at this exercise by sending "artful" errors, "clever" errors, "subtle" errors, and "faux," "ironic," and "meta" errors. Don't do any of that. I want full-on silly, stupid, and goofy errors. (Remember: there's no cheating in antiperfectionism work.) It's okay, however, to let your friends know what you're doing, and why—and if you encourage them to respond similarly, you'll be helping them to develop their own nonperfectionism!

Exercise 10. Nonperfectionism Around the House, and in Your Daily Life

Nonperfectionism anywhere will help you build nonperfectionism everywhere; and so don't hesitate to use the techniques we're discussing in every area of your life. Some of the most fun and inspirational moments I've had are when students or coaching clients tell me that, in the course of our work together, they've made progress on a goal we haven't even been discussing, like cleaning out the garage or signing up for a dating site. (Or, more seriously, signing up for a medical appointment they've been avoiding, or finally having a difficult conversation they've been postponing.)

Perhaps you've got a problem that is bothersome but not your primary concern. If so, use timed intervals, reframing, and the other techniques in this book to tackle it. Not only will you enjoy making progress, you'll strengthen your nonperfectionism for your art, business, or other vocation.[28]

---

[28] Reminder: as mentioned in the Vocabulary/Text Notes, I frequently distinguish between a job that you do entirely, or primarily, for money, and a "vocation" or "mission" that you do out of interest or passion.

19. Interrupting the Disempowerment Cascade

Perfectionism doesn't just show up and announce itself. ("Hello! My Name is Perfectionism.") Mostly what happens is that you start feeling guilty, scared, stuck, pressured, stressed, or otherwise bad about your work—a feeling that's followed, pretty quickly, by an urge to do something else. Instead of letting yourself get derailed, however, try writing out a dialogue between your Inner Perfectionist and Inner Compassionate Adult. Here's an example:

Inner Perfectionist (panicked): What's wrong with you? Why are you so lazy? This stuff isn't hard. Anyone could do it! Amy's already finished. Why can't you be disciplined like her? C'mon! If you don't get to work, you're gonna fail and everyone's gonna know you're a loser…and did I mention that the stuff you've already done sucks?

Inner Compassionate Adult (keeping cool): Okay, I hear you. And I really want to address the problem. But no name-calling, okay?

IP: But it's hopeless! We've got to stop being so lazy!

ICA (kindly but firmly): I mean it. We can talk about everything you want to talk about but you have to be respectful. And factual too, okay? No more hyperbole like, "It's hopeless!"

IP (glumly): Okay, I guess.

ICA: Great! Can you rephrase your concerns?

IP: Our project's in really bad shape and it's due on Friday.

ICA: Okay, I hear you. Do you have any suggestions?

IP: We could stay up all night working on it.

ICA: That's one option. But is it really a good idea?

IP: I guess not. We probably wouldn't get much done and it would wreck tomorrow.

ICA: Anything else?

IP: Not really…so what are your ideas?

ICA: Maybe we should delete that third section. It's got a lot of problems and I don't think we need it. What do you think?

IP (resignedly): Well, the result won't be as good, so that's kind of disappointing. But I guess this is an emergency and so we should delete it.

ICA: Great! We can always use it in another piece…and the project just got way easier, didn't it?

IP: I guess so.

ICA: Also, how about if we ask our supervisor for clarification on those confusing statistics?

IP (glumly): You know I hate asking people for help.

ICA: Oh, I know…but is that a good thing?

IP: He's going to think we're dumb.

ICA: Really? It's dumb to ask for help?

IP: I guess not.

ICA: And maybe Jeannie could help edit and proofread? We helped her out last month.

IP: I guess so.

ICA: We should probably also postpone our haircut and also Thursday's movie plans.

IP (a bit shocked at these "radical" suggestions): Really?

ICA: Sure! We can reschedule for next week. Everyone will understand.

IP (awakening to the fact that it would actually be great to reclaim that time): Yeah, I guess you're right.

ICA: The project seems a lot more doable now, doesn't it?

IP (now a bit optimistic): Yeah, I think so.

The more you use this dialoguing technique, the more you'll internalize the Inner Compassionate Adult's voice and problem-solving wisdom—until, eventually, you skip the perfectionism entirely and go right to the wisdom.

It's especially useful to do this dialoguing at times you think you've "failed." At such times, the perfectionist voice tends to be ascendant and so you need to do everything you can to neutralize it.

Incidentally, the above example is short compared with many real-life dialogues. As with all the exercises in this book, be sure not to rush it.

19. Interrupting the Disempowerment Cascade

How to Stop Fighting Your Inner Perfectionist

Did you notice how, when the Inner Compassionate Adult refused to let the Inner Perfectionist bully and insult them, it set the stage for a productive conversation? That's no accident: "limits are love," as the parenting manuals say. When the Adult set some limits, it helped the Perfectionist manage their fears.

Also, did you notice how the Adult refused to accept the Perfectionist's fake solution of pulling an all-nighter? Many Inner Perfectionists have:
1. good general goals (do excellent work, meet deadlines, etc.)
2. terrible specific goals ("do the best work anyone has ever done on this kind of project," "succeed at all costs," etc.), and
3. ineffective (to say the least) solutions ("stay up all night," "take no breaks," "never ask for help," etc.).

That's a confusing mix but it's the Inner Compassionate Adult's job to respect and act on (1) without indulging in (2) and (3). Use the above dialoguing technique, and your Inner Perfectionist will eventually realize that your Inner Compassionate Adult is not only serious about achieving your goals, but has some good strategies for doing that. Then they'll relax and retire from the scene, taking your now-unneeded Inner Procrastinator with them.

20. Overcoming a Punishment Habit

Many people are afraid that if they stop punishing themselves, they'll lose whatever shreds of willpower they have. As already noted, however, many of us have been punishing ourselves, or been punished by others, for years or even decades: if punishment (e.g., harsh self-talk and deprivation) really worked, we'd all be superachievers by now. The truth is that many of us are productive in spite of the punishments we've endured, not because of them. As the 20th-century psychologist B.F. Skinner said, "A person who has been punished is not less inclined to behave in a given way; at best, he learns how to avoid punishment."

You'll probably pass through three stages as you work to overcome your perfectionism / punishment habit:

Mostly Perfectionist. You're still mostly perfectionist but occasionally catch yourself at it and self-correct to nonperfectionism.

Mostly Nonperfectionist. You're now mostly nonperfectionist, although you occasionally lapse into perfectionism during stressful times, or when you've made a mistake, or are in the midst of an especially challenging project.

Nonperfectionist. You remain resolutely nonperfectionist even during times you're tempted to "cheat" with a little harsh self-talk or deprivation. (Again, there's no cheating in antiperfectionism work.)

It's the bone-deep knowledge that perfectionism *never* helps that will enable you to move as quickly as possible through the stages.

Like any behavioral change, the shift to nonperfectionism can feel weird at first. And giving up punishments can feel especially weird, because:

1. We're so used to our punishments that they feel normal.
2. Society keeps telling us that our punishments are useful.

3. We often use punishment performatively to reassure ourselves and others that, even though we're not getting as much done as we'd like, we're still taking our work seriously.
4. We often use our punishments as a form of penance or atonement for perceived underachievement. (Another type of performance.)
5. The punishments themselves are a form of procrastination. (Sneaky!)

If you're having trouble kicking your punishment habit, ask yourself which of the above purposes, or others, it might be serving. (Journal about it.) That knowledge, combined with your obstacle resolution process (Chapter 9) and other tools, plus your foundational ethic of non-punishment, should help you liberate yourself from the habit.

Once you stop punishing yourself, however, you'll probably encounter yet another barrier to progress and productivity. Both procrastination and perfectionism are dramatic and noisy habits. (All that monologuing, justifying, rationalizing, denial, distraction, shame, blame, guilt, regret, remorse, etc.) When you start to give them up—meaning, when you start to be able to sit down and do your work with a minimum of fuss—the simplicity, ease, and quiet can be unnerving. Plus, you now have a lot more time on your hands (because you're no longer procrastinating) that you're not exactly sure how to use. Not coincidentally—because procrastination often is, or resembles, a kind of addiction, as discussed in Chapter 2—this is all pretty similar to what many addicts experience during the early stages of recovery.

You'll need to learn to tolerate all this weirdness, at least for a while. You'll especially need to make sure that it doesn't send you spiraling back into perfectionism and procrastination. Persevere gently—always gently—and the weird feelings, which are kind of like "perfectionism's last stand," should eventually go away. Meanwhile, time management (Part V) will help you to deal with the "problem" (not really) of "too much time."

Hopefully, you'll eventually decide, at some not-so-distant point, that, "Dammit, I am *not* going to treat myself badly anymore, no matter how badly I think I've screwed up! It's not worth it, it feels terrible, and it doesn't help a thing." That's when you'll know you've turned the corner away from perfectionism and toward a happier, brighter, kinder, more abundant, and more productive future.

Exercise 11

Think back on times you've shamed or otherwise punished yourself, and answer the questions below about the incidents. (Journaling works well for

PRODUCTIVITY IS POWER II

this exercise and you may also wish to discuss your answers with a friend or therapist.)
1. Were there unspoken motives underlying the punishments? Did you, for instance, punish yourself in an effort to demonstrate, to yourself or others, that you were serious about your work, despite your having been underproductive, or "failed" in another way?
2. How did the punishments affect you and your work?
3. What might have been healthier and more productive ways to respond to the situations in question?

21. How to Distinguish Between High Standards and Perfectionism

High standards are great and so are ambitious goals. But how do you know when you've crossed the line into unrealistic standards, otherwise known as perfectionism? This is yet another confusing area, but here are some guidelines:

Unrealistic standards are often realistic ones taken a bit too far. Right now, for instance, you might be capable of working for half an hour without a break, but not forty minutes. (Or even thirty-five.) Or, of writing two pages during a work interval, but not two-and-a-half. Or, of exercising for twenty minutes a day, but not thirty.

We all have limited time and energy. In addition, we all find some projects and tasks harder than others. Productivity work is all about getting real, especially about our all-too-human limitations. Sure: you can, and should, aim for improvement—that's called growth and it's a wonderful thing. But bashing yourself for not being where you'd like to be, or not progressing fast enough, is perfectionist.

Unrealistic standards are often the wrong standards. "To win at all costs" is not just a perfectionist goal, it's the wrong goal: doing your best, in a way that's congruent with your values, is better.

Perfectionistically trying to cram as much work as you can into every workday, either because you think you're supposed to or because you feel guilty taking some time off for yourself, is both inhumane and unsustainable. Better to do your time management (Part V) and aim for life balance.

Some people aim to never (perfectionism alert!) disappoint their loved ones, but it's better to have healthy boundaries—which invariably means disappointing them from time to time.

Obviously, I'm dichotomizing: you can win *and* live your values, work hard *and* have a balanced life, and please others *and* have a healthy relationship with them. But one goal should be paramount, and perfectionists often choose the wrong one.

Unrealistic standards are often vague—and empty. Remember how poor Kayla (Chapter 12) wanted to write a novel that offered "as true and nuanced a portrait of her family's...history as she could?" But what does that phrase actually mean? When it comes to perfectionist goals, there's often no "there" there—and it's that very vagueness that can trap the creator in an endless quest to figure out a way to somehow do better.

Even when a perfectionist goal is more concrete, however, there's often still a problem. Recall that Kayla also wants her novel to be "well respected." Let's assume that that means something like, "getting published by a top publisher and getting favorable reviews in a few prestigious literary magazines." First of all, we're back in the realm of overidentification, narrow definition of success, and overfocus on product and external recognition. Kayla's perfectionism will be an obstacle to her being able to even finish her book, much less finding success in the marketplace.

And what if Kayla does actually manage to finish her book and achieve her publishing success? Meaningful as these achievements are, it's far from assured—especially given the vagaries of creative careers—that they will translate into the kind of sustained career boost she's probably hoping for, or the deeper reward of a long-term sense of satisfaction and fulfillment. And if Kayla's achievements don't, in fact, meet her expectations, she's liable to wind up even more disappointed and disillusioned and demotivated than ever.

Ironically, it's process-focused and holistic nonperfectionism that offers us our best chance of achieving not just success, but the deep rewards that we hope will come with it—and that's true even if we aren't lucky enough to "strike career gold."

Expecting a certain outcome when you don't have all the information or control needed to achieve it is unrealistic, and therefore perfectionist. As noted in Chapter 13, we never have all the information or control—so keep your focus on your process and your expectations moderate.

Unachievable goals are grandiose, and therefore perfectionist. *Really?* I hear you say. *Why would anyone set an unachievable goal? That doesn't even make sense.* You're right, it doesn't. But people set unrealistic goals for themselves all the time, and you've done it too, if you've ever...

- Taken on an overly ambitious project, as discussed in Chapter 13.

21. How to Distinguish Between High Standards and Perfectionism

- Taken on more work than you could possibly accomplish, given your time and other constraints.
- Expected any outcome to be 100% positive. (See Chapter 23.)
- Expected yourself to stay healthy and productive while stinting on self-care.

There are many other examples. Many working parents, for instance, bash themselves when they are working and not with their kids, and also when they are with their kids and not working. Basically, they're bashing themselves for not being in two places at once, which is pretty grandiose. (And deeply unfair.)

Finally, and most confusingly:

The same goal can be perfectionist and nonperfectionist at different times. It can be more reasonable to expect a good outcome for certain projects rather than others. Or, at certain times of your life more than others. (Obviously, if you're dealing with serious personal problems—or, even a good development that takes up a lot of your time and attention, like a wonderful new romantic relationship—that will have an impact.) **That's why your final and most important clue as to whether you've crossed the line into perfectionism is this: perfectionism hurts.** If you're feeling stressed, pressured, or otherwise bad about your work, that means you've probably crossed the line. Stop what you're doing and do some journaling and obstacle resolution work (Chapter 9), so that you can return to compassion as soon as possible.

22. Learning the Art of Failure

The most important time to put your Inner Compassionate Adult in charge is when you've "failed," experienced a rejection, or had some other kind of setback. It's a natural temptation, during such times, to get self-critical, but nonperfectionists have better ways of coping. They know that:

Everyone fails. It's an ordinary part of life. In fact, successful people probably fail more than most because they take more risks. To be precise: they're successful both because they take the risks and because they react productively—meaning, in the ways described in this chapter—to the inevitable failures.

Failure is essential. You learn things from it that you never would from success, including resiliency, humility, how to compromise, and how to play defense. (As well as, of course, how to avoid or correct the mistakes that caused you to fail in the first place.) As adrienne maree brown says in *Emergent Strategy*: "I don't experience failure much these days; I experience growth." Which brings us to...

There's no such thing as a complete failure. Nearly all failures yield at least some positive outcomes and even the worst are valuable learning opportunities. The more serious a failure seems, the more important—and healing—it is to actually sit down and list those positives.

Most failures turn out to be unimportant. This includes even some that seem awful at the time. A week later, you wonder what you were so upset about, and a month later, you've forgotten the entire incident.

A surprising number of failures turn out to be lucky breaks. Like when you get rejected for a job you later realize wouldn't have been a good fit. Or rejected romantically by someone you later realize wouldn't have been a good partner.

A failure can also clear the way for you to start on a new and better path. As the Chinese philosopher Lao Tzu put it, "New beginnings are often disguised as painful endings."

Only rarely is one person entirely responsible for a failure. So, yeah, maybe you made some decisions that contributed to your small business's demise. But maybe financial constraints, a poor economy, changing industry standards, or changing consumer preferences also played a role. And if you're a BIPOC or queer person, or a woman in a male-dominated industry, then discrimination might have also contributed.

Or, maybe you experienced a personal or family crisis that took precedence over your business. **Prioritization isn't procrastination**, although perfectionists who feel guilty over "not being able to do it all" frequently confuse the two.

Okay, so maybe your novel didn't sell because it had some flaws. But maybe it also didn't sell because the book publishing industry is both shrinking—so that, year after year, there are fewer opportunities to get published—and faddish. ("Vampires are big, this year—you got any vampires in your book?")

And, again, maybe discrimination played a role.

It's also important to remember that **ambitious plans are ambitious for a reason: the goal is hard to achieve**. This point may seem obvious but it's easy to forget when perfectionistically blaming yourself. The U.S. Bureau of Labor Statistics estimates that around 20% of small businesses fail in their first two years, 45% during their first five, and 65% during their first ten.[29] So, while it may seem like "everyone but me" is living their entrepreneurial dream—in part, because the media loves to hype the success stories—that's far from the case.

It's also unrealistic, and therefore perfectionist, to expect yourself to succeed at an ambitious goal the first time around, or even the second or third time. Sure, sometimes lightning strikes—but, far more often, entrepreneurs, artists, performers, novelists and others build their success over years, sometimes with the help of a "big break" but often without.

It's important to acknowledge all the causes of a failure, not to negate your own responsibility, but so that you don't take on an unjust burden of shame. (To be clear, you shouldn't feel ashamed even in situations where

---

[29] https://www.investopedia.com/articles/personal-finance/120815/4-most-common-reasons-small-business-fails.asp. It's interesting, by the way, how several of the causes of business failure that the article lists correlate with perfectionist characteristics, including a lack of planning, inadequate resourcing, an unwillingness to seek help, and rigidity.

you did do something wrong: see below.) This is perhaps even more crucially important in the work world where employees often get blamed for failures they didn't cause—for instance, when someone is given responsibility for a project, but not the resources or authority needed to accomplish it. (Or, when senior executives make poor strategic decisions, but it's the line workers who get laid off.) This is not only devastating when it happens, but can lead to years or even decades of shame.

Situations where you did your best but still got a suboptimal outcome aren't failures. They're just life! Again: none of us ever has complete control over our outcomes.

You have to be really, truly willing to fail. These days, many people do, in fact, understand that, "you have to be willing to fail." But ask them what they mean by that and they'll say things like, "I just want to do a decent job," or, "I'll be okay if I'm anywhere in the top ten." The problem is that, even though these kinds of goals sound reasonable, they're still overfocused on outcomes. If you find yourself procrastinating, therefore, ask yourself if you're really, truly willing to fail, or just think you are. If you really are, then you'll be focused mainly on process and thinking only a little about outcomes.

What "being willing to fail" really means is that you are prepared to get an F, come in last, bomb, embarrass yourself, even. Obviously, we all hope that that doesn't happen *this time*, but it probably will happen eventually if you're taking some good risks. When it does, it probably won't even feel so bad if you're focusing on process, maintaining a proper emotional distance from the work, not being shortsighted, etc.

Last, but definitely not least, the most important thing nonperfectionists know about failure is that regret, remorse, shame, blame, and other negative reactions are pointless. So skip them! **The *only* useful way to respond to a failure is to: (a) analyze what went wrong, (b) make amends to others if needed, (c) make a plan to do better in the future, and (d) move on.**

Or, as the spiritual teacher Ram Dass put it, "It is important to expect nothing, to take every experience, including the negative ones, as merely steps on the path, and to proceed."

Exercise 12

Examine some of your "failures" from the standpoint of the information in this chapter. Were they really complete failures, or did they actually have some positive aspects? Has time revealed them to be less important than they initially seemed? Were you really completely responsible, or did others, or bad luck, play a role? Write out your answers and, if desired, discuss them with a friend, mentor, or therapist. Hopefully, after you're done, you'll feel more at peace with these incidents.

23. Learning the Art of Success

Do we really have to learn how to succeed? Isn't success simply the party that comes after all the hard work? Not quite. Success is great and I wish you lots of it. But it can complicate things, and even lead to situational perfectionism (Chapter 15). Lao Tzu, who obviously thought a lot about the whole success/failure thing, put it pretty plainly when he said, "Success is often as dangerous as failure."

Perfectionists often gloss over their successes—or, worse, reframe them as failures (Chapter 13). But nonperfectionists are careful to recognize and celebrate their successes. Doing so is not only fun, it helps to neutralize perfectionism and fixes your successes in your memory so that you can call on them when needed for motivation. ("Okay, I'm feeling stuck, but I remember that just a few weeks ago I felt equally stuck. But I persevered and everything turned out fine. So I guess I'll persevere now, too.")

Recognition involves four steps:
1. Write down a list of the parts of your project, or the aspects of it, that succeeded. Be sure to define "success" as broadly and holistically as you can: remember, from Chapter 13, that it's not just about the outcome.
2. For each of those successes, list the skills and personal qualities—e.g., intelligence, patience, kindness, courage, nonperfectionism, persistence, resourcefulness, etc.—that helped you to accomplish it.
3. List any problems you solved and the skills and personal qualities you used to do that.
4. List any barriers you overcame and the skills and personal qualities you used to do that.

You'll also want to consider the parts of the project that didn't go so well. As noted in the last chapter, do that nonjudgmentally and then move on.

By **celebrate**, I mean, first of all, taking some time to feel truly proud of what you've accomplished. (As written up in your "recognition" document.) If you want to go beyond that and treat yourself to a dinner out, a new outfit or piece of gear, or some other splurge, go for it. Obviously, the magnitude of your celebration should roughly correlate with the magnitude of your success—maybe save the big celebrations for the big accomplishments—but it's okay to be a little generous with yourself to the extent that your budget allows.

Be sure to recognize and celebrate even your "small" and partial successes. For one thing, they're often bigger and more important than they seem. Even something as "small" as reviewing your notes for a project you've been avoiding can take real courage, so why not recognize and celebrate that? (Especially since doing so will empower you to take further steps.) Also, recognizing and celebrating your small and interim successes can help you to stay motivated throughout the course of a long project. In fact, big successes, as such, don't really exist: they're just accumulations of small ones. George Eliot didn't cough up her fantastic epic novel *Middlemarch* all at once like a hairball, for instance: she created it one paragraph, page, and chapter at a time. And before she even started it, she had successfully written many smaller works, and had also succeeded at a lifetime of study and other preparation.

Of course, the minute you do try to celebrate your small successes, your Inner Perfectionist will likely show up to scorn you as unambitious, self-indulgent, etc. As always, treat them with compassion but don't let them abuse you, and don't take their advice.

While understanding that recognition and celebration are important, nonperfectionists also know not to take things too far. In particular, they know that your successes shouldn't be a source of exaggerated pride (e.g., "I'm king of the world!"), self-justification ("That'll show 'em!"), or professional legitimacy ("After I'm published, then I'll be a *real* scholar."). Your successes should also not be a route to popularity, love, sex, status, or any other form of personal validation. All of these attitudes are extremely overidentified—and so, to some extent, this problem is theoretical, because people who view success in these kinds of ways tend to be much too terrified of failure to do their work.

The Costs of Success

Nonperfectionists also know that:

Success leaves you busier. Many successes create more work: for example, when you get a grant and then have to do the project. Success also can be a magnet that draws new people and projects to you. Don't get me wrong: these are excellent problems to have. But they're still problems. (See Part V for solutions.)

Success raises the stakes. It causes you to ask questions like: "What if my next project doesn't turn out as well as this one?" Or, "Now that I've gotten my dream job,[30] what if I can't handle the responsibilities?" Or, "Now that the newspaper is publishing my editorial, what if I get blowback on social media?" Or, "Now that I've gotten a date with this person I've been crushing on, what happens if it doesn't work out?" These kinds of questions are all natural, and I'd actually be worried if you *weren't* asking them. But dwelling on your fears or, even worse, letting them dictate your behavior, won't get you far. Instead, **always answer your rhetorical questions.** What *will* you do, for instance, if your next project doesn't turn out so well? (And how do you define "well?") Or, if you can't handle your new job's responsibilities? (And which responsibilities are we talking about?) Answering these types of questions is not only empowering in and of itself, it gives you a chance to avoid, via planning and consultation with mentors, the potential problems.

Last, but definitely not least,

Success always involves at least some compromise, loss, or sacrifice. Some examples:
1. It's practically impossible to have a notable success—be it in business, art, activism, or another field—without saying "no" to numerous social, family, community, or other commitments. (Section V can help you figure out where to draw the line.)
2. Your success may require that you live in a big city, thus quashing, at least temporarily, your dream of living in the mountains. (Or vice versa: maybe you settle for a less-ambitious career so that you can live in the mountains.)
3. Do well at your career and you may become a public figure, thus losing some of your precious privacy.

---

[30] Watch the labeling! "Dream job" is the kind of label that can lead to a lot of expectations—and perfectionism.

4. Find a wonderful romantic relationship and you lose the ability to mostly do whatever you want, whenever you want, without having to consult anyone else.

You need to be aware of these kinds of losses because it's easy to get caught off guard by them; also because fear of them—a.k.a., fear of success—is a major cause of hoarding and procrastination. **Now we see that procrastination's "purpose" isn't just to protect us from potential criticism or rejection (Chapter 2), but potential loss.** That's a powerful double punch, so be sure to use your journaling, discussions with mentors, counseling, and other techniques to not just identify your potential losses, but figure out how to minimize or prevent them, and how to cope with those remaining. Step 1 is to stop dichotomizing: in the above examples, you can still go to some social events, perhaps live near the mountains if not actually in them, still (through judicious use of social media) retain some of your privacy, and still retain some of your autonomy. You also want to do the work of mourning and accepting those losses you can't avoid so that you can proceed wholeheartedly and unambivalently with your work. Journaling and discussions with friends (or a therapist) work well for this, or you can go deeper via a spiritual discipline like Buddhism or a secular one like Acceptance and Commitment Therapy. Russ Harris's book *The Happiness Trap* is a good starting point for the latter, and there are also therapists who specialize in it.

Despite the complex nature of success, including all the attendant losses, I hope you have a lot of practice coping with it!

Exercise 13

Journal about a project you've been procrastinating on to see if any success related fears and potential losses might be contributing to that procrastination. If so, keep journaling to defuse the fears and minimize the losses, and also to mourn those losses that are inevitable. (If necessary, consult a friend or therapist.) When you're done, hopefully you'll be able to approach your work with less procrastination and ambivalence.

24. Overcoming Ambivalence

Ambivalence is when you're caught between two or more contradictory goals or motives. Ambivalence about small things—"Should I have a doughnut or a muffin, I can't decide!"—is no big deal. (Unless it becomes chronic, in which case it's Quasiproductive Procrastination. See Chapter 5.) But ambivalence about bigger things like your work, relationships, career, or identity can be awful. You're stuck in an exceptionally uncomfortable and confusing place, often doing the one-step-forward-two-steps-back kind of behavior that is so frustrating to you and those around you.

Here are some examples of ambivalence:
- Your family wants you to spend the holidays with them but you would rather do something else. But you are reluctant to have that conversation, and so wind up procrastinating on your travel plans until all the cheap flights are gone.
- You hate your job but don't want to go through the hassle of finding another. So you stay put, only keep getting less and less motivated and focused on your work until, eventually, your supervisor fires you.
- You've taken on a community project you don't have time to do. So you procrastinate on it, hoping some time will magically open up. Only that doesn't happen and so you wind up, finally, handing in only a part of what you promised to do, thus disappointing everyone involved, including yourself.
- Remember how Eric (Chapter 1) knew, at the end of his first semester, that he needed to take a break from school, but signed up for the second semester anyway? Ambivalence.

24. Overcoming Ambivalence

As these examples show, ambivalence is a disempowered—and, often, passive-aggressive—response to pressure that is characterized by indecision, dithering, and busy work. Yup: we're talking Quasiproductive Procrastination big time. Two important things to keep in mind, however, are that:
1. Although the ambivalence is, like all forms of procrastination, a disempowered reaction, it also, as discussed in Chapter 11, represents the best part of you: the part that is fighting for freedom and authenticity and self-expression, and against bullying and coercion.
2. We're often ambivalent not just because others are pressuring us, but because we at least partly agree with their viewpoint—so that, for instance, while you don't really want to go home for the holidays, a part of you thinks you should.

Solutions to Ambivalence

One solution to ambivalence is to **get clear on your relationship boundaries**—and, in particular, on your obligations and responsibilities to the various people in your life. (More on this in Chapter 45.)

Also, **work on your perfectionism**. Dichotomization is an obvious trigger for ambivalence since it can cause you to reduce all of your options to two equally extreme and unappealing opposites—so that, for instance, you think you either have to spend all of your holiday with your family, or none of it. Or, even worse, that you have just one unappealing option, like poor Eric thought he had. (To maintain the pretense of being in school even after it was clear he wouldn't be able to finish his degree.) Perfectionism can also cause you to dismiss good, or even excellent, solutions that are right in front of you, while you carry on a quest for a mythical perfect solution with no negative aspects. Philosophers call this the "Ideal Solution Fallacy," and it's a close relative of the Nirvana Fallacy (where you compare things to an idealized version of themselves) that I discussed in Chapter 14—which, no surprise, can itself also cause ambivalence.

Find a mentor. Often we're ambivalent because we don't have enough information to make a decision. The person who hates their job, for instance, may not know how to go about finding another. (Or may erroneously think that they're not qualified for anything else, or that, "there aren't any good jobs out there.") Because that lack of knowledge is often buried underneath layers of emotional turmoil and interpersonal strife, the ambivalent person may not actually be aware that that's the problem. So go ahead and do your obstacle-resolution process (Chapter 9); then discuss the situation with a mentor, therapist, or other expert.

Watch out for situations where you're having both halves of a conversation in your own head. It's a very common form of Quasiproductive Procrastination, and a recipe for ambivalence.

Finally, **learn to take the long view** (Chapter 16). It's always tempting to want to avoid the pain of dealing with a bad job, disappointing career, difficult relationship, or other problem. But ask yourself whether you want to be stuck with the problem for the next few months, years, or even decades, especially knowing that it's only likely to get worse. Ask yourself, also, if you want to develop a habit of avoidance and denial, or one of problem-solving. Hopefully, it's the latter, because...wait for it!...you don't want to be ambivalent about tackling your ambivalence.

Exercise 14

Look back at an incident where you were ambivalent about something in your work or personal life. List the ways that (a) perfectionism and (b) unclear interpersonal boundaries might have played a role. Also, think about how you responded to your ambivalence, and what might have been a better way to respond—and how you'd like to respond to future, similar episodes of ambivalence.

> *Okay, we're done with perfectionism! Thanks for hanging in there. In Part III, we'll discuss a nonperfectionist work process called the Joyful Dance. It's as much fun as it sounds, and I can't wait to introduce you to it.*

Part III

Joyful Work

25. Introducing the Joyful Dance

The goal is easy, effective, and joyful productivity, which is really nonperfectionist productivity. To see why, let's look at the way many perfectionists tend to work. They're relentlessly linear, for one thing: always trying to do everything in what they consider to be the right order. When writing a piece of fiction or nonfiction, for instance, they try to do all the research before moving onto the outlining, all the outlining before starting to write, etc. And when they do, finally, start to write, they trudge through the manuscript from beginning to end, trying to perfect (red alert!) each sentence, paragraph, and page before moving onto the next.

Linearity isn't just boring, it's precarious. Get stuck, during a linear process, and you really are stuck, because the one direction you think you can move in is blocked off.

Linearity also invites a kind of do-or-die perfectionism. ("Okay, so I finished Section 3. Now it's time to start Section 4, AND I'D BETTER GET IT RIGHT!")

The fundamental problem is that linearity undermines your creativity. **Creativity is really a kind of conversation** between you (your knowledge, ideas, thoughts, beliefs, and perspectives) and:

- your subject matter (including past and present experts)
- collaborators (including your colleagues, coworkers, mentors, audiences, and others), and
- your materials, processes, and techniques.

Like many conversations, these "creative conversations" work best when information flows freely in many directions. This includes backward, by the way, because creativity is also fundamentally an act of discovery. The things you discover later in a creative conversation can, and probably will, illuminate some of the insights and ideas you discovered earlier, making you want to go back and change them. As the poet May Sarton once helpfully observed, "Revision is not going back and fussing around, but going forward into the process of creation."

Creativity, in other words, is organic and holistic—pretty much the opposite of a linear process.

For all of these reasons, **nonperfectionists work nonlinearly**, which means that they work on whichever parts of the project they feel like working on at the moment. Also, they work on whichever *stage* of the project they feel like working on. Organizing, writing, editing, etc.—they combine it all into one big jazzy jumble, switching among them with ease. (This includes sharing the work, which, as discussed in Chapter 16, nonperfectionists do early and often.) There's just one stage that you should omit from your jumble, and that's research, which, as discussed in Chapter 5, is a common vehicle for Quasiproductive Procrastination. It's okay—and desirable, as I'll be discussing in the next chapter—to write, outline, etc., while doing research, but you should avoid slipping into research when you're supposed to be working on the other stages. (More on how to handle research in Chapter 32.)

I call this jazzy, jumbly, nonlinear work process the Joyful Dance because that's what it feels like when you use it: a joyful dance through your work. And I call the perfectionist way of working the Dreary Slog because that's pretty much what it feels like. (Yup, I'm labeling and dichotomizing to get my point across. In real life, no one is 100% Dancer or Slogger.) The Joyful Dance supports and catalyzes your creative conversations, and so, when you use it, your work goes easier and faster, and is a lot more fun. You're also far less likely to get stuck when you're Joyfully Dancing because "getting stuck," to a Dancer, simply means that it's time to switch over to another part of the project. (Which Dancers do without fuss or drama.)

Remember Chapter 4's point about how empowerment means having good options? The Joyful Dance is all about that. When Dancing, you get to choose, at every moment, not just which part of your project you want to work on, but how you want to work on it. By contrast, the Dreary Slog only ever offers you the same bad choice: to keep working on whatever it is you're currently working on until you get it "right." Notice how your personal preferences and situation—not to mention, the specifics of the project itself—don't even enter into it.

25. Introducing the Joyful Dance

Is the Joyful Dance actually joyful, though? Sometimes! Other times, it's "merely" interesting, satisfying, fulfilling, or fun. Don't knock it: these are excellent work experiences to have. What I can promise you is that **the Joyful Dance will maximize your odds of not just an easy and effective and fun work process, but a good outcome.** When you work nonlinearly, you're like a surfer on a beach with some great waves, each wave being a bit of inspiration comin' atcha. You see one, rush over to it, grab it, and ride it. Then, when it peters out, you look around and see another great wave, rush over, grab and ride it. Then another and another. You keep doing that throughout your whole work session. What fun! And look how much you're getting done.

Meanwhile, your poor Slogger friend is standing forlornly with their surfboard on the section of the beach where they think the next great wave is supposed to hit. Waiting...waiting...waiting...

Get Random!

Nonlinearity can feel weird if you're not used to it. But give it a whirl and you should soon see the advantages. This randomizing technique should help:

Assign a number to every section of your project (assuming they're not already numbered, as in book chapters). Then roll some dice[31] and work on (using Timed Work Intervals, see Chapter 6) whichever numbered section you rolled. If you get bored or stuck, roll again and hop on over to the new section and work on that. Or, if you feel suddenly motivated to work on a section—say, because the current section gave you an idea for it—hop on over there and start working on it. Hop around as much as you like until you've completed your interval, while resisting, as always, the temptation to judge your output.

Randomization works not just because it's fun, but because it subverts perfectionism. Instead of, "Now it's time to do Section 4, and I'D BETTER GET IT RIGHT!!!!!" you're all: "Hmm, just rolled a '4.' Not sure what I want to do with that section but I'll play around with it and see what happens." And what often does happen is you get a good creative conversation going.

---

[31] Even fancy dice are pretty cheap (and fun): check out places that sell gamers' supplies. For free dice, ask a gamer friend for a set they're no longer using, or grab the dice from an old board game that no one's using. And, yes, I know that you can download a random number-generator app for your phone, but *puhlease* no phones while working.

Randomization also works well with another technique for avoiding perfectionism, **chunking.** That's when you break a big project down into manageable chunks and focus on one at a time. A chunk could be a page or paragraph of a written document, a subroutine or module of a computer program, or an element of an artistic project. Go ahead and assign numbers to your chunks, then roll those dice.

Assigning numbers to your **to-do list** entries, and then rolling the dice to work on those randomly, is another great technique for getting stuff done.

You probably won't need to keep rolling those dice forever, by the way. Soon you'll learn to ask yourself, when you sit down to work, "What do I feel like working on right now?" And then you'll get right to it. Then, when you feel like you're tapped out on that section, or simply have the urge to work on something else, you'll automatically (again, without fuss or drama) switch over to a new bit. And you'll keep working, and switching, and working some more, until you reach the end of your interval.

But you should feel free to return to the dice if you ever feel yourself slipping back into linearity.

26. Speed It Up!

We all want to work faster, but make sure you're aiming for the right kind of speed: not the frantic and stressful kind that depletes you (and triggers procrastination), but the cool and steady kind that you can maintain for long periods without getting bored or tired. (What marathoners call their stride.) The kind of speed, in other words, that helps you get a lot of work done while also supporting your creative and other objectives.

Pretty much every technique in this book will help you achieve some of that speed, but to reach your personal maximum, you'll need to do what the marathoners do and organize your life and work around that goal. Below are some tips for doing that:

Do your time management (Part V) to make sure that: (a) you're getting enough sleep, exercise, and other self-care, and (b) you have as much high-quality time as possible to devote to your work. ("High quality" means time when you're alert, energetic, and relatively free from interruptions: see Chapter 46 for more on this.)

Eliminate interruptions. As discussed in Chapter 5, they're more "expensive," time-wise, than we realize. (Breaks are okay and necessary: see Chapter 33.)

Get comfortable, not just because that helps with speed, but also because, as discussed in Chapter 9, a lot of procrastination begins in the body.

Optimize your workspace. If you need quiet, find quiet. If you need the room to be at a certain temperature, find that. And if you need a window, or no window, find that. Don't settle for a space that's not a great fit because that will be just one more obstacle to doing your work.

Work alongside other focused workers. Many people work faster in a group setting, assuming that those around them are themselves focused on their work. If you're one of them, find yourself a library, café, or coworking space full of quiet and industrious people, and enjoy the boost you get from working alongside them. (As discussed in Chapter 6, there are also apps that can help connect you with others.) Please note, however, that the more you overcome perfectionism, the easier you might find it to work alone—and if solo work becomes your preference, then you shouldn't hesitate to do that.

Do some preemptive obstacle work (Chapter 9) before starting projects so that you can eliminate obstacles while they're still small—or, better yet, prevent them from occurring in the first place.

Plan your large or complex projects. It doesn't have to be a super-detailed plan. (And shouldn't be: don't turn your planning into Quasiproductive Procrastination.) Just write down a few milestones and deadlines. Planning not only helps you stay on track, it helps you visualize your project as a whole, which further boosts your productivity.

Reduce your project's scope. As discussed in the "What to Do If You've Got an Urgent Deadline" section at the front of this book, and also in the "Cut it Out" section of Chapter 28.

Stick to "process" goals. As discussed in Chapter 7, even some seemingly benign goals, such as "to do good work" are actually perfectionist; and so the only goal you should aim for is, "to finish my work interval while remaining nonperfectionist throughout." Beyond that, creativity is an organic process that takes time, so you shouldn't get bogged down trying to perfect a bit of work in the moment. A good process-related maxim—and one of the most calming things you can tell yourself, especially in the midst of a difficult project—is, **"I don't have to fix this problem right now. I'll have time to fix it later."**

The most effective and efficient work method, generally speaking, is to:
- work on a bit of your work until the well runs dry (you lose interest, lose steam, run out of ideas, etc.); then...
- work on other pieces while you let that first bit "marinate" in the back of your mind. And then,
- return to the first bit when you're charged up with some new ideas and enthusiasm.

(See, also, the discussions of trial-and-error in Chapter 28, the importance of not forcing or controlling the work in Chapter 29, and Quickdrafting in Chapter 30.)

26. Speed It Up!

Do a Pilot or Prototype; then share it with your audience for feedback. When writing a novel, for instance, send an early chapter to your editor, agent, or alpha readers just to make sure you're on the right track.

Ditto for projects in the visual arts: share some early sketches, storyboards, etc., with those who can give you excellent feedback.

When writing a computer program, first create a "bare bones" version, without any bells and whistles, just to make sure it does the basic things it's supposed to do; then show it to your supervisor or client for comment.

Along with gaining you some good feedback early on when it's most useful, doing a pilot also helps you nip problems in the bud. It's also a great anti-hoarding technique that should boost your confidence (and speed) for the remainder of the project.

Do some of your work on the day you're assigned a project. (Or, the day you think it up.) That's often when your enthusiasm and creativity are at their peak.

Alas, many people not only don't do this, they do the exact opposite and wait till the last minute to start, either because they're procrastinating, aren't managing their time well, or both. This almost guarantees that they'll wind up rushing through their work and having a miserable time. (And probably getting a worse outcome.)

Do a bit of work on all your projects most days. Productivity-wise, there's nothing worse than a "cold start"—meaning, when you return to a difficult project after a long break. While you should do most of your work in stretches of half an hour or more—that's both efficient and often needed for concentration (more on this in Chapter 46)—in between those stretches, do some short intervals of around five or ten minutes on any projects that you're not focusing on that day. This will not only help you keep the material fresh, it will leave you with less work to do later on. (Because the intervals, although small, do add up.)

While working, **keep a light touch and a light heart**, even if the work itself is serious. You may have difficult problems to solve, and serious points to make, and intense scenarios to explore, but try to do it all while keeping at least some emotional distance. This can be difficult, so if, despite your best intentions, you find yourself getting caught up emotionally, try journaling about the situation or discussing it with a friend, mentor, or therapist.

The above techniques are humane and effective alternatives to trying to shame yourself into working faster—which, in any case, is only likely to backfire. But let's take a deeper, more philosophical look at the whole "speed" question.

Make Haste, Slowly

Perhaps you've heard of the global Slow Movement, which urges that, in an age of technological speedup, we all become more deliberate and mindful about our various activities. The movement has spawned several sub-movements, including Slow Food, Slow Travel, and Slow Parenting.

Let's talk about Slow Work. Over the years, I've spoken with teachers in many fields, including science, the arts, engineering, the building trades, and automobile mechanics. They've all said the same thing: that one of their major challenges is getting their students to slow down enough to focus on the details of their work. Students tend to rush, in large part because they don't realize how long it takes to do good work. The truth is, it can take a shockingly long time, especially when you're still learning. (And even after you're more experienced! I still can't believe how long it can take me to write a "simple" blog post.)

Working too fast yields not just a sloppy result, but a difficult and joyless process. Plus, it's an obstacle to learning and growth. You need to slow down enough to not only get the details right, but understand why they're right. In fact, **whenever you sit down to do your work, it should be with the attitude that, "I have an infinite amount of time to get this done."** This will slow you down to your natural, relaxed, unhurried pace—the pace at which you can focus on the details. Now, of course, I know that you don't actually have infinite time. But, in yet another of those happy productivity paradoxes, pretending that you can can actually speed your work because it minimizes perfectionism and procrastination, thus liberating your creativity. As Carl Honoré says in his book *In Praise of Slowness*, an overview of the Slow Movement, "Performing a task in a Slow manner often yields faster results."

I can't emphasize this enough! There have been countless times, during the writing of this book, when I caught myself thinking, "This bit of writing is taking too long! If I spend this much time on every page [or paragraph, or sentence], the entire book is going to take forever!" Whenever I caught myself thinking that way, however, I intentionally adopted the opposing view: "I have unlimited time to work on this." And at the very moment I did that, my stress and pressure would melt away, leaving me relaxed and eager to do my work—which then invariably went much faster than it had before. This example also shows that **you must always counter perfectionism with a strong opposing stand.** Weak neutrality isn't sufficient! If I had responded to my internal pressures by saying, "I'll give myself a day to write this paragraph. That's a generous amount of time." I still would have felt pressured and constrained. (This is an experiment you can try for yourself.)

This "infinite time" trick also aligns with Anne Lamott's technique, from her writing guide *Bird by Bird*, of viewing your work as if through a "one-inch picture frame"—meaning that you focus on just the tiny bit of it that's in front of you, without worrying at all about the rest.

To recap: you want to work with focus and intention and commitment, but *not* with any sense of urgency. Obviously, there will be times when you're facing an imminent deadline and need to step on the gas. But the more you learn to, as one of my mentors put it, "make haste, slowly," the better and faster you should be able to work, and the fewer of those stressful urgent deadlines you should encounter.

At the same time you're doing your Slow Work, be sure to choose relatively short and simple projects. This is especially important when you're relatively new to the work and/or are working to overcome your perfectionism, for five reasons:

All projects are harder than they seem. Even a seemingly "simple" project will probably be hard enough.

Keeping things simple allows you to focus on the details while still completing your project on time.

Novices and those with perfectionist tendencies tend to overstuff their projects, so keeping things simple will help to counteract that.

As noted in Chapter 7, quantity (finishing lots of small/simple stuff) will help you build your quality.

"Finishing" is a vital skill, and working on smaller/simpler projects will allow you to practice it more often. (More on this in Chapter 31.)

What if you want to do longer and more complicated projects? No problem! Just build up to them gradually. Every new project can be as long and complicated as you like—until you start feeling scared, pressured, under-resourced, or otherwise perfectionist.

If, while you're keeping it small, a critical internal voice pops up saying stuff like, "Wow, you're really unambitious! Step it up!" I believe you now know exactly who that voice is and how you should handle their advice.

27. Get Fresh!

Ideas are like cookies: better when fresh. A fresh idea is rich with meanings, associations, connotations, and other "flavors." It's also soft and malleable, so you can use it in different ways. But old ideas, like old cookies, go stale, losing a lot of their flavor and becoming stiff and brittle. When a Slogger uses a linear process that involves "doing all the research and organizing first, and only then starting to write," they're doing the intellectual equivalent of constantly eating stale cookies. (Yuk! No wonder they procrastinate.)

So use your ideas when they're fresh. You do that by **doing your writing and other "output" work in parallel with your planning, research, and other preparatory ("input") steps.** Let's say you're doing some research for your novel and find a useful nugget of information. Don't write it on an index card or note file with the idea of later transferring it into your manuscript. Just plunk it right down into your manuscript in the spot you think it best fits. Then start writing and editing around it. (Obviously, always be sure to use proper citations. Never plagiarize.) Then, when you run out of steam with it, go back and do some more research until you find your next useful nugget.

As noted in Chapter 5, however, you shouldn't do the opposite and research when you're supposed to be writing or doing other output work, because research is a prime vehicle for Quasiproductive Procrastination.

Doing your writing and other output work in parallel with your research and organizing and other inputs also yields a more integrated, polished, and well-thought-out product—and the bigger the project, the more obvious these qualities will be.

27. Get Fresh!

Picture two writers with research-intensive projects. One does all the research first; then finds themselves close to their deadline with little or nothing written, and an intimidating mountain of material to sort through.

The other has been writing all along; and now, close to their deadline, has a creditable draft, parts of which are probably already close to finalized.

Which writer would you rather be?

28. Wizard-Level Problem-Solving

The problem, often, is problems. We can be happily chugging along doing our work and then be stopped cold by one. Our tendency, at such times, is to sit there and ponder, á la Rodin's famous sculpture, "The Thinker." Most of us, however, aren't that great at abstract thought and so our efforts don't yield much—at which point, there is a strong temptation to flee via procrastination.

To do better, you need to first understand that most of what you're doing, when you're working, is making decisions. It doesn't matter whether you call those decisions, "writing," "programming," "business planning," or something else: it's still just decisions. Even a "small" project can require hundreds: a few large, some small, many tiny. Some you make consciously while others are automatic. (But weren't always: while you can now write simple sentences and do simple math automatically, those tasks would have involved some very big decisions back in elementary school.)

In between the decisions is the time we spend implementing, or doing what we decided to do. But decision-making is usually a much bigger part of our projects than we realize, and even when we're implementing, we're still usually making some decisions.

The next thing you need to understand is that **what we refer to as a "problem" is just a set of decisions that requires more time and effort than most.** (Again, watch the labeling.)

So, a key to working fast is to make efficient decisions—and a key to that is, again, nonperfectionism. Dichotomizing, pathologizing, rigidity, impatience, etc. are all obvious barriers to decision-making. Perfectionism can also convince you that none of your solutions are any good, thus getting you stuck on looking for "the right one."

28. Wizard-Level Problem-Solving

One of the saddest things about perfectionism is how it can suck the joy out of a potentially fun process. Think about it: many people solve problems for fun via crossword puzzles, sudoku games, mystery novels, and brain teaser puzzles. Why should the problems you solve for your work be any different? This may sound silly if you're used to viewing "work" and "fun" as opposites, but, as I've discussed at various points in this book, you absolutely do want to approach your work as play.

The foundational solution for speeding up your decision-making, and hence your problem-solving and overall productivity, is nonperfectionism. Here are some others:

Trial and Error. Instead of sitting there and pondering, go ahead and try out some solutions. This gets you out of the realm of abstract thought and into the far more productive (and fun) one of using your skills. (You're "thinking by doing," in other words.) Sooner or later—and probably sooner—you'll come up with a solution that works.

The key to successful trial and error is to not censor yourself. The whole point is to give yourself the freedom to experiment and play. But if you start pre-emptively shooting your ideas down—say, as "unlikely to work" or even "silly"—that defeats the whole purpose. (I guess I don't need to tell you which part of yourself is likely to do that.) Also, "unlikely" or "silly" ideas often turn out, with just a little tweaking, to be winners.

Trial and error is another example of Chapter 7's idea that quantity yields quality. Generally speaking, the harder your problem is to solve, the more trials it will take to solve it. But solutions can often come surprisingly quickly. Or, to put it another way: our problems often aren't as tough as our inner perfectionist would have us believe.

To be clear, **trial and error isn't just a problem-solving technique, but your main work method.** It's what writers do when they Quickdraft, for instance (see Chapter 30), what visual artists do when they sketch or storyboard, and what coders do when they use iterative development techniques. Trial and error is the main "format" of your creative conversation, in other words—and it's also no coincidence that it provides you with lots of empowering options (Chapter 4) for proceeding with your work.

Write for Help. Write an email to someone summarizing the problem and asking for help. Doing this gives you some emotional distance from the problem while at the same time allowing you to look at it from a fresh angle. The amazing thing is that, often, you don't even have to send the email: just writing it is enough to get you unstuck. (As discussed in Chapter 10, asking for help, all by itself and regardless of any response that you receive, is empowering.) But if you want to go ahead and send it, feel free.

Cut it Out! As noted earlier, novice creators, and even experienced ones who are perfectionist, tend to overstuff their projects. And guess what? It's often that excess that clutters things up and otherwise causes problems. So try removing the problem bit. (Possibly saving it for another project.) This advice applies not just to entire sections of your work, but to individual sentences, phrases, and even words.

It's amazing how often this trivial-seeming action of cutting works, and how good it feels. There's something deeply satisfying about giving a troublesome part of your project the boot. One caveat, however: don't cut out of fear. Some of the most valuable work happens when you arrive at a mess, take a deep breath, and then dive in and really try to work it out. A general guideline for when to cut content is: if there's a problem with your central thesis or theme, try working it out. But if the problem is a tangential bit, go ahead and cut. (Obviously, keep a backup in case you change your mind.)

The worry, when you cut, is that the project is going to wind up too short. This is often both a perfectionist worry—because perfectionists mistrust "easy" success—and a pragmatic one: sometimes there's a minimum word count or other requirement you have to meet. Sometimes you can solve that by gathering the more interesting cut bits into a section devoted to "secondary issues" or "topics for further research and discussion." Even when you can't, however, there's probably some part of the work that you can expand, which brings us to...

Expand It. Often a bit of work won't come together because we're trying to cram too much information into too few words. So another technique is to expand the troublesome bit. First, copy it into a new window so you have lots of room to experiment and play; then let your creativity take charge. Often, the piece will open up in interesting and fun directions.

This also works well for visual projects: the bit that's not fitting may be the nucleus of a fantastic, new project.

Finally, for tough problems that are resisting any solution...

Start Over, this time letting the work find its own way. Impatient and rigid perfectionists are often horror-struck when I suggest this—and I do agree that it does sound very inefficient—but productive people do it all the time. And you know what? The new version usually goes way faster. That's often because: (a) after all your prior attempts, you finally do know what it is that you're trying to do or say, and (b) you're less controlling this time around. (See the next chapter to learn why trying to control the outcome isn't helpful.) Please note, however, that **there's a difference between occasionally starting a difficult project over from scratch and constantly starting all of your projects over from scratch because you're afraid to**

finish. The former is great, while the latter is a seriously self-sabotaging perfectionist behavior that I discussed in Chapter 13.

29. How to Get, and Stay, Inspired

Poets, philosophers, and others have been pondering the mystery of inspiration for thousands of years, but all "being inspired" means is that you're ready and motivated to do the work. And all "being uninspired" means is that you're not—yet. So what does it take to be ready? A few things, including an understanding of the process you need to follow, confidence, a detailed knowledge of how to do the next couple of steps, and abundant preparation. Let's discuss each individually.

An Understanding of the Process. This may seem like a no-brainer but many people who think they know what they're doing actually don't. They're operating from a mix of hunches and guesswork, perhaps with a dash of shallow media advice (e.g., "10 Tips for Writing Your Novel" or "How to Succeed as a Musician") mixed in. What often happens, in such cases, is that the person gets mired in a lot of Quasiproductive Procrastination—e.g., busy work, redoing the same work over and over, over-researching, etc.—that gives them the illusion that they're making progress. On some level, though, they know they're stuck; and their doubts keep growing until, one day, they're tipped over the edge by a "failure," harsh criticism, or other crisis. Or, perhaps they get a new job or relationship, or experience another major life change, that consumes all their time and attention, and allows them to passively quit their project (and dream).

You need to think very carefully about whether you're in this situation if you're: (a) working in isolation, and especially without mentors, or (b) not using a plan with deadlines.

Confidence. Even if you understand your process, it's easy to get discouraged if you don't feel confident. You obviously need confidence in your skills but it's even more important to have confidence in the availability of help. Most of all, you need confidence that, if you make a reasonable effort, you'll have a reasonable chance of success. (As mentioned in Chapter 4, futility may be the most disempowering emotion.) Things have never been easy for creative people but it may be especially tough these days, when monopolistic corporations have severely curtailed writers', artists', musicians', and others' ability to reach their audiences and make a living. The solutions are to:

1. create a realistic strategic plan (if your goal is to make a lot of money from your writing, romance novels are a better bet than poetry, but even with romance you need to know what you're doing);
2. find your niche and work to excel at it (being the go-to person for a specialized need or product is still a viable small business strategy);
3. learn from mentors who have figured out how to thrive (as best as possible) within the exploitative system, and
4. join, or help organize, a union.

Of course, some goals are harder to achieve than others—and it always helps, if you're going after one of the tough ones, to maintain an expansive and holistic, otherwise known as nonperfectionist, view of success. For example: "Even if I don't achieve my primary goal, I still will have accomplished something worthwhile. Also, I will have learned many useful things, and had a great time doing this project."

Along with understanding and confidence, you also need to know **how to do the next couple of steps *in detail*.** Otherwise, you might get stuck on one of them, or on your current step. (Because you're aware, at least semiconsciously, that you don't know how to proceed, and are afraid of failure.) Good ways to test whether you know enough are to: (a) write the steps down in detail, and (b) try explaining the steps to someone else—even your dog or cat. Any holes in your knowledge should quickly become apparent. (If you're working without a mentor you should assume you don't have all the information you need to proceed.)

Finally, to be inspired, you need to have done **Abundant Preparation**. Here, again, are the typical steps of a writing project: conceptualization (a.k.a., brainstorming or idea generation), research, organization / outlining / plotting, first draft, revisions, and sharing the work. **Notice how the step most people think happens first, "first draft," actually happens more than halfway through.** It takes a lot of work even to be able to do a first draft! If you get stuck, therefore, try going back and spending more time on the conceptualization, organization, and research stages, and you should regain your inspiration. Similar advice applies to other fields: if you're stuck, go back and review the fundamentals. When you do that, it often turns out that you don't understand them as well as you think you do, and that, once you correct that problem, your work goes much more easily.

The word "inspiration" literally means "breathing in," and that's exactly what you're doing during the early stages of your project: "breathing in" the work of experts past and present, which you then combine with your own ideas and insights in your creative conversation. But if you rush through those early stages, as many novices and perfectionists do, because they are in a hurry to get to what they consider "the real work," you starve yourself of the inputs needed for inspiration, pretty much ensuring that your work will be a grind.

Know Thyself and Thy Motivations

Even if you do have the understanding, confidence, detailed knowledge, and preparation needed to proceed, you can still find yourself getting stuck. In such cases, try answering these four questions:

(1) **Am I being perfectionist?** I know, I know: again with the perfectionism! But it will rob you of your inspiration faster than just about anything. Ask yourself, especially, whether you're overfocusing on outcomes, or being overidentified, grandiose, impatient, mistrustful of success, and/or rigid. If the answer is yes, then use your reframing, dialoguing, and other solutions to overcome that.

(2) **Am I doing this project for the right reasons?** Especially, ask yourself if you're doing it to try to impress others. That's a sign of overidentification, among other possible problems. I can usually tell when someone is in this bind because their project will be over-serious, over-complicated, and over-intellectualized—e.g., "My novel is about death as a metaphysical protest and ecstatic reaction, in the vein of Tolstoy and Dostoevsky, and with subthemes invoking Gogol and Chekhov." Also, it's pretty clear, usually, that the person's heart really isn't in the topic. (Also see Chapter 13's discussion of overambitious projects.)

(3) **Am I ambivalent for other reasons?** Perhaps your project revisits some difficult personal or family history, or explores challenging issues such as war, genocide, domestic violence, or animal cruelty. (All real-life examples from people I've worked with.) If so, try the solutions in Chapter 24, and always remember that empowerment means creating more good options for yourself—including the option to not work on a project, or with a topic, if you don't feel fully ready to do so.

(4) **Am I trying to force the work?** Imagine that you're having a fun conversation with friends. Then, all of a sudden, someone starts to talk over everyone else, and insist that the discussion be held in a certain way, and arrive at a specific conclusion.

Not so fun or productive anymore, is it?

It works the same way with the creative conversation: the moment you try to control it, you shut it down. Often, when we do this, it's because we're aiming for a certain quality standard like "excellence" or "comprehensiveness" or "originality." That's admirable but repeat after me: You Can't Force the Work. As the French novelist Gustave Flaubert put it, "Success is a consequence and must not be a goal."

Therefore, a final thing to ask, and answer, when you're feeling stuck or uninspired is, "Am I trying to force the work?" Or, alternatively: **"Am I trying to control the outcome?"** or "Am I trying to dominate the creative conversation?"

If this turns out to be the problem—and it often does—then politely ask your Inner Perfectionist (and ego) to step aside so your creative process can take its natural, organic course. Of course, this may mean that the work moves in a direction you hadn't intended. That's creativity for you! Every productive person has probably experienced that and, honestly, that's kind of what you want. (Fiction writers are always talking about that amazing, but admittedly somewhat unsettling, moment when, "the characters take over.")

30. How to Write Like a Pro

Writing is a paradox. On the one hand, it's an incredibly common activity that many of us feel we mastered way back in elementary school. On the other, it's really easy to get stuck when doing it.

Clearly, there's a lot more to the "simple" act of writing than many of us think. The main problem is that, along with the intellectual and creative challenges we expect, writing presents a whole set of challenges that we don't, including solitude, sedentariness, and—let's face it—monotony. (All those endless rounds of putting down words and taking them out again.) Add to all that the fact that it often takes a lot more work than we expect to create a good piece of writing, and it's no wonder many people struggle.

Fortunately, there are some professional writers who are taught how to deal with all that, and whom we can learn from. They include journalists—who often must make weekly or even daily deadlines—and the genre writers of science fiction, fantasy, romance, mystery, etc., many of whom write a book (or more!) a year. Below is a suggested writing process that incorporates many of the techniques used by these highly productive writers. Even if you're not a self-described "writer," but simply someone who is expected to do some writing on the job, they should work for you.

(1) **Stay grounded.** Some people approach their writing like it's some kind of holy mission: an overidentified and grandiose approach which, needless to say, isn't helpful. In his memoir *On Writing*, Stephen King suggests you view your writing as, "Just another job like laying pipe or driving long-haul trucks." It's good advice!

(2) **Stay playful, even when writing serious stuff.** Writing, like all creativity, demands freedom and a light touch—and that's true even when what you're working on is highly serious and/or intellectual. That doesn't

mean that you should be all ha-ha jokey when writing about, say, climate change or genocide, but only that you shouldn't fall into the trap of thinking that you're supposed to be actively depressed while doing so. A little emotional distance from your subject matter is often a good thing.

Of course, it can be difficult to maintain that distance. If you do find yourself getting depressed or otherwise affected by what you're working on, talk to a friend, mentor, or therapist. And don't feel obligated to tackle a subject if it seems too emotionally challenging: your mental health should be your top priority.

(3) **Daydream productively.** Recalling the last chapter's discussion of abundant preparation, another secret of prolific writers is that they invest heavily in the foundational "conceptualization" step of the writing process. Charles Dickens, for instance, would often take, "a vigorous three-hour walk through the countryside or the streets of London…'searching for some pictures [he] wanted to build upon.'"[32] I imagine him, while walking, pondering the next scene in *Oliver Twist* or *Great Expectations*, then coming upon a real-life scenario that helped him put everything in focus.

Ursula K. LeGuin once told an interviewer that, after waking up, she spent around 45 minutes lying in bed and thinking before having "lots of" breakfast, and then sitting down to write for around five hours.[33] We can assume she used her early-morning thinking time to fuel her ideas for her writing, just as she used the big breakfasts to fuel her physical energy.

I'm guessing that Dickens kept a notepad handy while walking so he could jot down his inspirations. And perhaps LeGuin kept one by her bedside. (One way you know you're in a creative person's home is that there are notepads and/or piles of scratch paper everywhere.) I similarly recommend you carry a notepad or use your phone's voice recorder when daydreaming away from your desk. But also try conceptualizing at your desk by journaling about what you're working on and the specific problems you're trying to solve.

(4) **Use props.** Some writers work to a music playlist that's thematically related to whatever it is they're writing. Others create mind maps, flowcharts, or timelines. And still others create posters, scrapbooks, maps, collages, and even faux book covers. Props can be fun to create, and very inspiring and motivating. So have fun creating some! Only don't do it when

---

[32] From Mason Currey's book *Daily Rituals*, which includes lots of fun descriptions of how famous creative people did—or, in some cases, do—their work.
[33] https://www.openculture.com/2019/01/ursula-k-le-guins-daily-routine-the-discipline-that-fueled-her-imagination.html

you're supposed to be writing because that would be Quasiproductive Procrastination.

(5) **Create your "shitty first draft."** The idea of a shitty first draft was popularized by Anne Lamott in her book, *Bird by Bird*. She describes it as follows: "The first draft is the child's draft, where you let it all pour out and then let it romp all over the place, knowing that no one is going to see it and that you can shape it later. You just let this childlike part of you channel whatever voices and visions come through and onto the page."

Lamott also describes shitty first drafts as self-indulgent, boring, stupefying, incoherent, hideous, and, "almost just typing, just making my fingers move." She also notes how perfectionism—which she calls "the voice of the oppressor"—is the main obstacle keeping you from completing your shitty first draft because you can't tolerate the shittiness. Interestingly enough, when I ask perfectionists to describe what a shitty first draft looks like, they typically say something like this: "Well, it's rough in places, but it's mostly organized and the major points are there..." Perfectionists' shitty first drafts, in other words, are like nonperfectionists' almost-final drafts! For the record, truly shitty first drafts—and this includes my own—are pretty incoherent and disorganized. So make sure you're comfortable creating truly shitty, shitty first drafts.

Once you've written your shitty first draft, it's time to move onto my favorite part of the writing process...

(6) **Quickdraft.** During writing productivity classes, I sometimes ask the trick question, "How many drafts should you do of a paper or other piece of writing?" The students who are creative, academic, or business writers usually answer something like, "three" or "five" or "ten." But the journalists always answer, correctly, "As many as it takes." But you need to know what they mean by a "draft": not a slow, linear slog through the chapter or other chunk of writing you're working on, but a kind of nimble dance through it, during which you stop to make only the easiest and most obvious edits.

The goal, in other words, is to do lots and lots of fast drafts. Now, sooner or later, while you're doing that, you're going to come across a bit you feel like focusing on, and you absolutely should do that. That feeling is called "inspiration," and you don't want to waste it. When it passes—meaning you've written or edited as much as you can, at that moment, on that bit— simply return to your quick work.

Then, when you reach the end of the chapter (or other unit you're working on), you return to the beginning and start over.

30. How to Write Like a Pro

Your writing process, then, consists of alternating fast and slow work, with you shifting as desired between those two modes without hesitation, fuss, or drama.

You keep doing all that until you finish your Timed Work Interval (Chapter 6).

I call this process Quickdrafting and it offers some terrific advantages, including that it's:

- Nonlinear and fresh. You can start anywhere within your piece that you want, and are also free to stop and focus on whichever bits you'd like.
- An active, easy, interesting, and fun way to write, so you don't get bored.
- Preserving of your energy, so that you can work longer without getting tired.
- Generative. Each time you do a Quickdraft, you gain ideas and insights that fuel the next.
- Accelerative! Meaning that, the more Quickdrafts you do, the faster the remaining ones should go. (In contrast to linear work, which tends to first slow down, and then bog down.)

Quickdrafting is particularly useful for big projects because it helps you to comprehend your project as a whole, leading to more speed and a better, more integrated product. Quickdrafting also helps you to avoid the kinds of rabbit holes, tangents, and other time-wasters (see Chapters 31 and 32) that are easy to fall into when you overfocus on one part of a big project. Your early Quickdrafts will, in effect, be "sketches" for your final written product. Just as visual artists do preliminary sketches to make sure they've got their overall composition right before starting to fill in the details, writers can also benefit from doing that.

How many Quickdrafts does it take to complete a paper or other piece of writing? (*Not* a trick question, this time.) The answer varies depending on the project. It could be as high as ten, twenty, or even more—but don't panic: a nonperfectionist can do dozens of Quickdrafts faster than a perfectionist can do even one "Slowdraft." (Assuming that they even finish that one.)

If you get stuck while Quickdrafting—and at some point, on most projects, you probably will—use the techniques in Chapters 28 through 32 to get unstuck and resume your Quickdrafting. Especially, don't forget to show your drafts early and often to avoid hoarding (Chapter 32).

(7) **Stay calm and patient—i.e., nonperfectionist—when receiving criticism.** The moment you get comments back from a colleague, coworker, friend, editor, or alpha or beta reader, is one of the most fraught in the entire writing process.

The first pitfall is emotional. Obviously, you want to set your perfectionist ego aside and evaluate those criticisms and suggestions nondefensively, with an open mind.

After you decide what changes you want to make in your work, there's another challenge, which is that it can take a surprising amount of work to integrate even small changes into an existing text. Sometimes that's because you have to do a lot of writing and editing around a change, or because a change triggers more changes, and then more, etc., in a kind of domino effect. And sometimes it's because a change requires that you view your text in new and unfamiliar ways. In all cases, the key is not to panic. Start just by recording, right in your manuscript, notes about the changes you want to make. (I often list them in bullet point format.) Then start Quickdrafting around those notes, working with even more patience than usual.

(8) **Remember the goals.** As discussed in Chapter 26, these are: (a) to do the best you can at the moment, and (b) to finish your interval.

(9) **Remember the rewards**. It's noteworthy that, despite writing's many inconveniences, so many people are drawn to it. That's probably because it offers numerous and profound rewards, including meaning, growth, transcendence, transformation, and joy. As Flaubert famously put it, "Writing is a dog's life, but the only life worth living." And Toni Morrison once said that, while she didn't particularly enjoy the act of writing, "Without it, you're stuck with life."[34] (The same can be said of all creative and intellectual pursuits, of course.)

Staying mindful of the rewards can help you stay motivated throughout the course of your projects, and also help you build satisfaction and joy throughout your career.

---

[34] Quoted by writer Fran Lebowitz in this interview: https://freshairarchive.org/segments/humorist-fran-lebowitz-writing-and-not-writing-0.

31. Navigating the Project Life Cycle

Just as humans go through life stages—infancy, childhood, adolescence, adulthood, etc.—projects also go through life stages. In this section, I discuss each stage individually so you can anticipate its characteristic challenges and prevent them from stalling your projects.

The **Honeymoon** is the very beginning of your project—literally, the first few minutes or hours, or (for bigger projects) days or weeks. At this stage, the project exists mainly as a glorious golden vision in your head—and what you are probably envisioning is not the product itself, but how amazed and impressed others will be when they see it.

Even when you do envision the process, it's probably all smooth sailing, with few, if any, serious problems.

This golden vision is super motivational, and so, for a while at least, you work like gangbusters. But then, inevitably, the vision starts to crack and tarnish as you realize that:

- The work you've done so far isn't great. In fact, it's pretty bad. (Our early efforts almost always are—refer, again, to Anne Lamott's "shitty first draft.")
- The project's got some serious problems that you don't know how to solve, or even if you can solve them. And even if you can...
- The project is going to turn out very different from, and not nearly as good as, the golden vision. (Because nothing could possibly turn out that well.) And, finally,
- You still have an enormous amount of work to do.

Welcome to the **Anti-Honeymoon**, the stage of peak disappointment, disillusionment, and demotivation. It's the stage at which many people abandon not just projects, but careers, businesses, relationships, etc. English Literature fans will recognize it as the "Slough of Despond" from John Bunyan's classic 17th century allegory, *The Pilgrim's Progress*.

What's really going on is...you guessed it...perfectionism. The Honeymoon/Anti-Honeymoon cycle reeks of overemphasis on product, a narrow definition of success, overidentification, grandiosity, shortsightedness, impatience, pathologizing, and pretty much every other perfectionist characteristic. The key to coping, therefore, is to moderate your perfectionism and, especially, your expectations. Optimism at the start of a project is great, but avoid grandiose fantasies that will almost inevitably trigger a backlash of disappointment. Also, shitty first drafts and other early attempts almost always are "bad," so why even bother with that demotivating label? Just let your work be your work, especially in its early stages.

When the Anti-Honeymoon does arrive, keep cool and keep working, always keeping in mind that **the problem isn't your work, but your perfectionist attitude toward it.** (Just as, in *The Pilgrim's Progress*, the Slough consists of the Pilgrim's, "fears, and doubts, and discouraging apprehensions.")

Also, double down on your other solutions. Bunyan's protagonist, the pilgrim Christian, finally escapes from the Slough with the assistance of, "a man whose name was Help," hint, hint.

Get past the Anti-Honeymoon, and you'll soon enter the **Vast Middle**. If the Honeymoon/Anti-Honeymoon combination and Home Stretch (see below) each represent around 10% of your project, that leaves 80% for the Vast Middle. (That's vast!) The real problem, however, isn't the Vast Middle's vastness, but the fact that, much of the time when you're in it, you don't feel like you're making progress. In the midst of what can feel like endless rounds of trial and error that seem to be going nowhere, it's easy to get discouraged.

The solution, again, is to keep your cool and keep working—keeping in mind that **the "Vast Middle" is just another name for "doing the work."** Joyful Dancers and process-focused people in general don't actually mind the Vast Middle: it's only those who are overfocused on product—or, I guess, late on their deadlines—who see it as something to be rushed through.

Hang out long enough in the Vast Middle and eventually something great happens: you start to see the faint outlines of where you're going. Other ways of describing this exciting moment are: you start to discover what it is you're trying to say; your creative conversation starts to home in on a conclusion; your project starts to gel; and your meaning starts to emerge from all the chaos. Your work will probably get easier at this point, and it should continue to get easier, until you eventually arrive at...

...the **Home Stretch**, where what's mostly left to do is formatting, proofreading, and other relatively easy polishing. Many people enjoy this stage: just be sure not to enjoy it too much and get stuck there, because that's a common form of Quasiproductive Procrastination. (Also see the discussion of Fear of Finishing in the next chapter.) Avoid that trap, however, and you soon should experience...

The Finale. A mere moment in time but a deeply satisfying one. Take a moment to acknowledge and celebrate your achievement before moving promptly onto...

Sharing a.k.a., handing the work in. After you do, don't sit around and wait for the outcome: start working on your next project. (As discussed in Chapter 15.)

Later on, of course, comes **handling the feedback**. As discussed in previous chapters, remember not to take it too much to heart. Enjoy your "successes," learn from your "failures," and move on.

How to Handle "The Question"

Sooner or later, someone's going to ask you about the progress of one of your projects. If you're lucky, the inquiry will be phrased something like this: "So, how's it going?" If you're not so lucky, it will probably be more along the lines of one of these: "Still working on that thing?" "Haven't you finished it yet?" And, worst of all, "What's taking so long?"

Let's agree that, regardless of the form of the inquiry, the asker probably means well. But the last three phrasings are all perfectionist. (Not to mention, rude!) So how to handle them?

First, **be nonperfectionist**. Obviously, if you yourself are impatiently overfocused on product, or are devaluing the progress you've made (an example of negativity), then having someone ask about your progress is bound to be painful. So, keep your focus on your process and remember that many projects that seem to be "not going well" or "going too slowly" really aren't: they're just in their Anti-Honeymoon or Vast Middle stage.

Next, **instead of trying to justify or defend yourself, educate**. For instance: "Actually, novels typically take a few years." Or, "My editor says I'm right on track." Often, however, before we can educate others, we have to educate ourselves—and here, once more, mentors can really help. Acclaimed writer of massive biographies, Robert A. Caro, tells this story in his autobiography *Working*:

> I was bothered, too, by the length not only of the manuscript [of his book *The Power Broker*, about New York City "master builder" Robert Moses], but also of the time I had been working on it.
>
> That was the thing that made me doubt the most. When I had started, I had firmly believed that I would be done in a year, a naive but perhaps not unnatural belief for someone whose longest previous deadline had been measured in weeks. As year followed year, and I was still not nearly done, I became convinced that I had gone terribly astray. This feeling was fed by the people Ina and I did know. I was still in the first year of research when friends and acquaintances began to ask if I was "still doing that book." Later I would be asked, "How long have you been working on it now?" When I said three years, or four, or five, they would quickly disguise their look of incredulity, but not quickly enough to keep me from seeing it. I came to dread that question…

Skip forward a few years: Caro has been given desk privileges in the New York Public Library's prestigious Frederick Lewis Allen Room, where he finds himself working alongside, among others, two of the 20th century's most celebrated biographers: James Flexner (author of a multivolume biography of George Washington) and Joseph Lash (author of *Eleanor and Franklin*, a big biography of the Roosevelts). One day, Caro looks up from his work to see Flexner watching him:

> The expression on his face was friendly, but after he had asked what I was writing about, the next question was the question I had come to dread: "How long have you been working on it?" This time, however, when I replied, "Five years," the response was not an incredulous stare.
>
> "Oh," Jim Flexner said, "That's not so long. I've been working on my Washington for nine years."
>
> I could have jumped up and kissed him [...] as, the next day, I could have jumped up and kissed Joe Lash…when he asked me the same question, and, after hearing my answer, said in his quiet way, "*Eleanor and Franklin* took me seven years." In a couple of sentences, these two men—idols of mine—had wiped away five years of doubt.

31. Navigating the Project Life Cycle

This anecdote also illustrates why it's important to have mentors who have accomplished the same type of thing you are trying to accomplish. None of Caro's journalist friends could give him the specific information and perspective he needed. It had to be biographers—and not just any biographers, but those whose goals, in terms of scope, quality, and ambition, were similar to his own.

In case you're wondering, not even fame and acclaim will put a stop to the perfectionist inquiries. Caro reports that he is still, "constantly being asked why it takes me so long."

Finally, keep in mind that **how you say something often communicates as much as, or even more than, what you actually say.** So, try to answer the difficult inquiries with confidence and optimism, even if you don't actually feel that way. (The first person you convince may be yourself.)

How do you ask after the status of someone's project without putting pressure on them? It's usually fine to ask, "How's the work going?" in a neutral tone. But don't ask if you're not prepared to really listen to the answer and respond with understanding and compassion.

It's even better to ask, "Is there anything I can do to help?"

Exercise 15

Think back on some of your projects that have gone past deadline, or otherwise taken longer than they might have. Did you spend too much time on one or more of the project stages? More generally, is there a stage that you particularly enjoy, like research or revision, and tend to get stuck at? If so, then recognizing the problem will hopefully help you avoid it in the future.

32. Avoiding the "Big Four" Project Derailments

Along with the project stage-related challenges I discussed in the last chapter, there are four other very common project derailments that you need to watch out for. They are "Beginning Bias" (and other forms of avoidance), Reckless Research, Fear of Finishing, and Boredom. I discuss each individually below.

Banish "Beginning Bias" and Other Avoidance-Related Problems

Beginning Bias is what I call the tendency some of us have to overwork the beginnings of our projects relative to, and usually at the expense of, the middles and ends. (Quasiproductive Procrastination in action!) Years ago, a professional book reviewer told me that she could always tell when an author had this problem because the beginning of their book would be much more polished than the rest, which obviously got done in a hurry after their editor told them to, "hand it in or else."

Beginning Bias is actually a subset of a bigger problem with the Joyful Dance, which is that, by giving yourself "permission" to nonlinearly work on any part of your project, you're also giving yourself "permission" to not work on any part. Especially, we tend to avoid those parts that are difficult, tedious, scary (e.g., a presentation, if you have a fear of public speaking), or collaborative (tricky even with great coworkers and colleagues, much harder with difficult ones). Even worse, the more we avoid a piece of work, the scarier it gets and the more we want to avoid it.

Chapter 25's Randomization technique can help with mild cases of Beginning Bias and other avoidance. You can also use a "semi-random" technique that ensures that you do at least some work on every part of your project. When writing this book, for instance, I made sure to devote at least some Timed Work Intervals to each of the five main sections every week.

For stronger cases of avoidance, I recommend a technique I call **Microintervals**. Every hour or so while you're working on the easier stuff, switch over to the scary bit and work on it for a very brief amount of time, like a minute or even thirty seconds. You might edit a sentence, research a math or science problem, or send out a quick email for a collaborative project. As always, don't judge your work. (Obviously, you shouldn't be expecting to accomplish much in a minute, anyway.) Then, return to what you were doing.

After a few Microintervals, the scary bit won't seem so scary anymore. You'll be able to do longer Microintervals, and then even longer ones. Then, eventually, the scary bit will become just another *un*scary part of the project.

Rein in Reckless Research

Research is a common vehicle for Quasiproductive Procrastination because:
- It can be endless. Even a seemingly small topic, once you start researching it, can open up in dozens of different directions. Plus, new source materials are constantly being created.
- Many people enjoy it. Rooting around in archives, or falling down an Internet "rabbit hole," is fun!
- Every project is different and so it's hard to come up with general guidelines for what, and how much, research you should do.
- You learn how to research your topic partly by actually researching it — which is why so many historical novelists and scholars, after finishing their research, wish they could start over from scratch. (And some do just that, starting over and over, and never getting around to the actual writing.)

Perfectionism, as usual, makes everything worse, because, along with the usual types of fear of failure, you now have the additional research-related fear of, "leaving something out." One solution to over-researching, therefore, is to build your nonperfectionism. Another, as discussed in Chapters 5 and 25, is to not do research during your writing and other "output" work intervals.

If you think you're slipping into Reckless Research, use your Obstacle Analysis, Timed Work Intervals, Microintervals, and other techniques to get back on track. And, as always, ask your mentors. In fact, it's a great idea to ask them, at the beginning of projects, what kinds of research you should be doing, and how much. Rest assured that these are not naive questions but pretty savvy ones that they themselves probably still occasionally ask their own mentors.

Finish Off "Fear of Finishing"

Finishing your work is important, and not just for the obvious reasons. You gain confidence from finishing and also learn valuable lessons, like how to persevere through the Vast Middle or at other times you're feeling unmotivated. Finishing lots of projects will also help you build your skills and knowledge—Chapter 7's "quantity yielding quality," again—and gain a sense of who you are as a creator and what specialties you'd like to develop (Chapter 43).

Finishing is a skill. You learn it the same way you learn other skills: by practicing. Start by finishing small and easy stuff; then work your way up to bigger and more difficult stuff. All the obstacles and barriers discussed in this book can cause you to quit your projects before they're finished, but developing a commitment to finishing, and a self-image as a "finisher," will help you to persevere through them. One way to do that is to learn to recognize and celebrate your finishes as you would any success (Chapter 23).

Being a finisher doesn't mean you have to finish every single thing you start. (Even professionals experience the occasional false start.) But you should finish most of them, and also have a really good reason for not finishing something. Above all else, you want to avoid becoming the poor shortsighted perfectionist who abandons project after project because they can't see past the ordinary obstacles and "bumps" (Chapter 13) .

Give Boredom the Boot

Boredom, in an otherwise interesting project, is often symptomatic of a deeper problem, like perfectionism. So, when bored, do some journaling to see if it might be masking fear, anxiety, impatience, or confusion. (Then, obviously, take steps to remedy the causes.)

Here's one of my favorite solutions for boredom, because it's so unintuitive: **slow down**. When we encounter boring stuff, our tendency is to try to blitz through it and finish as quickly as possible. Unfortunately, this pretty

32. Avoiding the "Big Four" Project Derailments

much guarantees a miserable work experience and an inferior result. Instead, try slowing down and savoring the details, and you'll probably wind up having more fun and getting a better result. You might even finish sooner, since attempts to blitz often lead to procrastination. (See, also, Chapter 26's discussion of slow work.)

Slowing down and getting more mindful helps with a wide range of "boring" or otherwise challenging activities, from exercise, to skills practice (like when a musician practices scales or an athlete does drills), to personal finance chores, to even dealing with a chronic health problem.

Keep in mind that, especially if you are a creative person, entrepreneur, or community activist / organizer, you want to cultivate as wide a range of interests as possible. That doesn't mean you need to have a passionate interest in every single thing, but simply to have as few as possible biases and aversions. (You don't need to be a passionate sports or opera fan to be able to listen intelligently and respectfully to a colleague, customer, or potential collaborator who is interested in those things.) As the Roman/Berber playwright Terence said, "I consider nothing human alien to me." So another solution to boredom is to be as open-minded as possible to new ideas, tasks, and experiences. (Try to reframe them, as discussed in Chapter 18.)

None of this is to say that, sooner or later, you won't get stuck with a legitimately boring task. If you can't decline or delegate it (Chapter 44), and if slowing down isn't entirely working, then do your best to settle in and stay focused, while also being sure to follow the most direct and efficient path to completion. (Don't perfectionistically do more than you need to.)

But what if you find your entire project (or job, or career) boring? Sometimes, that's a sign you're doing something for the wrong reasons (e.g., to please others). Or, perhaps you're in a rut, and still working on stuff that was interesting and challenging a few years ago but no longer is. (Time to make a change?)

Ditto for relationships. If you're bored with someone, ask yourself whether it's a relationship worth preserving.

If household chores and other time expenses (see Chapters 40 and 41) bore you, that's actually a good thing: a sign that you don't want to squander your precious time on trivia. In this case, you should "listen" to your boredom and do as few chores as possible. (Part V has solutions.)

Intellectually, creatively, and otherwise, always strive to follow your passions, and to live and work as much as possible among others who are following theirs.

Exercise 16

The next time you're stuck on a project, use journaling to answer these questions:
1. Which part of the project life cycle (from Chapter 31) is your project at? Does your answer add any clarity to the situation, or suggest any solutions?
2. Are any of the derailments listed in this chapter present? If so, which of the solutions offered will help?

33. How to Take Excellent Breaks

Breaks are the productive person's secret weapon. They're essential from both a health standpoint (especially if you're doing a lot of sitting and screen work) and from the standpoint of avoiding fatigue, stiffness, restlessness, and other mental and physical triggers for procrastination.

They're also great for problem-solving. Many people have had the experience of struggling with a tough problem, only to have the answer "magically" pop into their head while taking a coffee break or walking the dog.

Your Inner Perfectionist probably disagrees. For them, breaks are just so much wasted time. "If you *must* take one, *at least* make it productive," they drawl, with supreme condescension. You know: by doing some other work, or learning a musical instrument, or aerobically running up and down five flights of stairs. (All real-life examples people have shared with me.) Important Reminder: as per Chapter 19, you should empathize with your Inner Perfectionist but never take their advice.

Your breaks should be easy and enjoyable. Sure, pick out a few guitar chords if you want. Or, do a few dishes or fetch the mail. Or, even do some push-ups or pull-ups, if that's your thing. But no strenuousness, unpleasantness, intensity, depletion, deprivation, coercion, etc.

Unfortunately, many who avoid the trap of a productive break fall right into the trap of a screen break. (Social media, Web videos, gaming, television, etc.) Screen breaks have two very serious problems, the first being that you're still sitting and using a screen. The second is that most screen activities are engrossing and distracting by design, so once you start one you're at serious risk for getting sucked in. (And even if you do manage to avoid that, your ten- or fifteen-minute break will fly by, and you won't feel rested.) An easy way to resist the lure of a screen break is to keep your phone off while you're working, and also to work on a disconnected computer, as discussed in Chapter 6.

A final type of problematic break is the social break. A bit of casual conversation while waiting for your chai is fine. An intense online or in-real-life interaction that can suck you in, and maybe leave you upset or otherwise distracted afterwards, isn't.

The best breaks tend to be enjoyable, active, low-stress, and not intensely interactive or otherwise distracting. A walk, some stretches, a romp with an animal companion, some dancing (assuming you work at home or in another situation that offers some privacy), or some meditation are all great choices. As always, do what works for you.

As for the interesting question of how long your breaks should be, I recommend tracking your "Break Percentage": the percentage of time, out of your entire work interval, that you devote to breaks. While you're still working on overcoming your perfectionism, your Break Percentage might be 50% (equal time spent working and on break) or even higher (more time on break than actually working). That's probably not a number you're happy with, but keep the faith: as you get more and more nonperfectionist, your work should flow more easily, and your Break Percentage should drop. A good goal to aim for is around 20% (twelve minutes of break time out of each work hour, perhaps divided into two or three chunks). The number will probably vary depending on context, however, and, as always, you should do what works for you.

Finally, **learn to distinguish a true break from disempowerment and procrastination.** Many people, when they encounter a problem with their work, zip through the entire Disempowerment Cascade in an instant and then "decide" to take a break. They're not breaking, they're derailed! Instead, stay calm and use your obstacle-resolution (Chapters 9 and 10) and problem-solving (Chapters 28 through 32) techniques to resolve the problem, or switch—as always, without drama or fuss—to an easier bit of work.

So that's the Joyful Dance. Use it and you'll create, finish, and share more work than ever before—perhaps more than you ever thought possible. And you'll also enjoy your work more than perhaps you ever thought possible. But there are even bigger yields than that, because **once we learn how to easily work on the things that are truly important to us, we become more free to develop into our truest self, and to help others to do the same.**

The Joyful Dance, it turns out, is not just a tool for productivity, but for liberation and love.

Finish and share more of your work, and you'll start getting more feedback. Some of it will probably be positive, but some will probably be critical, judgmental, or even rejecting. Part IV tells you how to handle that.

Part IV

Resilience

34. The Many Forms of Criticism and Rejection

Criticism and rejection can take many forms. There's "classic" criticism: when someone has something negative to say about you or your work. And "classic" rejection, or denial of a request or opportunity.

Then there's all of these: bias, callousness, carelessness, condescension, contempt, deprecation, devaluation, dismissal, disparagement, labeling, marginalization, mockery, neglect, ostracism, ridicule, sarcasm, shaming, and tokenism.

And these: passive-aggressive withholding of information, time, or other support, and non-accommodation of reasonable requests.

(Throughout the rest of Part IV, except where specifically indicated, I use the words "criticism" and "rejection" interchangeably to refer to all of the above.)

Constructive criticism—meaning criticism that's useful, appropriate, proportionate, and sensitively delivered—is essential to learning and growth. Painful as it can be, it's a sign that others are taking you seriously.

But harsh, arbitrary, or otherwise *un*constructive criticism can be really destructive. You know how an oyster responds to an irritant, like a grain of sand, by coating it with layers of nacre, eventually creating a smooth and non-irritating pearl? We often do something similar with harsh criticism: "coat it" with denial and procrastination to protect ourselves from future hurt. (Denial is when you bury the hurt and pretend it's not there. Procrastination, as discussed in Chapters 2 and 14, "protects" you by making you and your work invisible.) This process continues until you have, not a lovely pearl, but an unlovely block—and I know that this happens a lot because frequently, in classes, after I mention a specific type of harsh criticism or rejection, a student will get one of those *Whoa!* looks and say, "I just realized that that happened to me and afterwards I never wrote another short story."

Or, "...I stopped applying for fellowships."

Or, "...I dropped out of school."

Or, "...I stopped looking for jobs in that field."

Of course, it can work the same way in our personal lives: after someone rejects us cruelly, we may stop approaching others for friendship or love.

I call any criticism or rejection that leaves you feeling ashamed, unfit, fearful, hopeless, and/or otherwise diminished, "traumatic." Kayla's harsh treatment by her workshop leader (Chapter 12) is one example, and also note how the public nature of his criticism contributed to her pain. I'll discuss the different types of traumatic rejections, and how to cope with them, throughout the rest of Part IV. First, however, let's discuss a piece of singularly useless advice that's often given to those hurting from a rejection: that they "toughen up" or "grow a thicker skin." It's lousy advice for at least three reasons:

First, it's vague. How, exactly, do you do that?

Second, it implies you're being weak, and is therefore shaming. In fact, it *literally* adds insult to injury. (Recall Chapter 15's story about the soccer dad who unintentionally wounded his daughter with a similar comment.) And third...

We—meaning society—don't need any more thick-skinned people. Thick-skinned people go around stomping on others' feelings and generally causing trouble. And it's simply not true that they don't feel the hurt of a criticism or rejection. They might be in denial about it, but the pain is there, causing them to suffer and, often, mistreat others.

The goal, in other words, isn't toughness, but resilience. You want to be open, alive, caring, and receptive, but also capable of coping with the inevitable hurts and disappointments. To achieve that resilience, it's helpful to understand why criticisms hurt, and why some hurt more than others.

Why It Hurts

If your cherished but somewhat out-of-touch parents tell you that they dislike your new hairstyle, you probably won't get too upset, and might even take it as a good sign. But if a fashion-forward friend says the same thing, it can really hurt.

The same criticism (or rejection) will hurt more or less, in other words, depending on who's delivering it. (Also recall poor Kayla, from Chapter 12, getting harshly criticized by the writer she admired.)

It will also hurt more or less depending on a few other factors, including:

- How much you care about the thing being criticized.
- How hard you worked on it.
- Whether the criticism occurs publicly (for instance, in front of a class or on social media).
- If you're criticized at a time when you're also coping with other difficulties.

The content of a criticism will also (obviously) determine its hurtfulness. The most hurtful criticisms tend to be harsh, cruel, and/or shaming. And the very worst tend to be personal attacks, such as, "Do you really believe those things you wrote in your essay?" or "What makes you think *you* can be a [fill in the blank]?" People sometimes say these kinds of harsh things in a caring or reasonable tone of voice, which can be confusing. But the pain is real—and, as usual, it's often the best and most caring people who tend to be the most vulnerable.

Bigoted or biased criticisms and rejections are also extremely hurtful—not to mention, violations of basic principles of social justice and, in some cases, illegal (if they cross the line into discrimination or harassment). Bias can also lead to internalized oppression, which is when you start to believe the bigoted view, thus limiting your sense of yourself and your potential.

Callousness is another common offense. It's when someone criticizes or rejects you without making a reasonable effort to minimize the hurt. Along with the pain of the criticism itself, it sends the additional painful message that you don't merit ordinary consideration and respect. Form letter rejections, especially for opportunities you were personally encouraged to apply for, or had to do a lot of work to apply for, are a common example.

Don't be fooled if a harsh or callous criticism comes labeled as "tough love" or "fun ribbing." It's still hurtful and irresponsible, especially if coming from either someone who says they care about you, or who has a professional obligation to support you (e.g., a supervisor or teacher).

Marginalization is likewise common. It's when your values, concerns, and/or achievements are trivialized, dismissed, treated as an afterthought, or ignored. Families, friends, and coworkers sometimes do it to group members whose values differ—so that, for instance, a family full of business people may do it to the one artist or activist in their midst. (Or, vice versa.) It's also often done passive-aggressively—meaning, that your family, etc., wound you by *not* acting or speaking—which makes it even harder to identify and deal with. An example would be when your group says nothing / asks nothing / does nothing about an important project you're working on, or about a recent success or failure you experienced.

Finally, we have **blindsiding**, which happens when we either don't expect a criticism, or don't expect it to be as harsh as it is. Because your defenses are down, blindsiding can be *very* painful and take a long time to heal. A common form of blindsiding is when someone whom you would reasonably expect to be on your side—like a parent, teacher, lover, or friend—attacks or betrays you. And you can also blindside *yourself* by expecting a success that doesn't happen. (Recall Chapter 13's discussion about how expectations are always risky.) Even when—especially when—all indications are that a project will succeed, always be prepared for the possibility that things won't turn out as you expect. As Luke Skywalker told the arrogant Emperor Palpatine, "Your overconfidence is your weakness."

Make no mistake: the above behaviors can hurt, especially if they happen repeatedly.[35] In situations like these, you're often caught between either sticking up for yourself and your values (and being seen as an irritant or source of conflict), or staying quiet and not advocating for yourself. The phrase "caught between" indicates your disempowerment and perceived lack of good options. Beyond all that, you can get DARVO'd. DARVO is a useful acronym coined by psychologist Jennifer J. Freyd to describe a common response to accusations of abuse: the abuser Denies, Attacks, and Reverses Victim and Offender.[36] An example would be when you get upset because a family member is being hurtful, and they turn it around and say that you're the unreasonable one and are hurting them.

I'll offer some empowering options in the next chapter, but in the meantime Exercise 17 should help you process some harsh criticisms and rejections you've experienced.

Exercise 17

1. Journal about some criticisms and rejections you've experienced. See if you can link them to any procrastination, perfectionism, or blocks you might have experienced, or may still be experiencing.

---

[35] Research by psychologist Naomi I. Eisenberg and colleagues found that rejection and other forms of "social pain" activate the same brain areas as physical pain. See: https://ncbi.nlm.nih.gov/pmc/articles/PMC3273616/.
[36] https://dynamic.uoregon.edu/jjf/defineDARVO.html

34. The Many Forms of Criticism and Rejection

2. For each incident, list any elements of context (e.g., the critic's status, or the time or place of the incident), content (e.g., personal attack or bias), or delivery (e.g., harshness or callousness) that increased the hurtfulness. Hopefully, identifying these amplifying factors will help you to further process the event and defuse any lingering pain. If it's still painful, however, you might want to talk to a friend or therapist.

35. How to Cope

The goal, as stated in Chapter 34, is resilience—and, fortunately, you already know much of what you need to achieve that, because **90% of resilience is nonperfectionism.** Perfectionists are like burn victims: sensitive to even the slightest "touch," i.e., criticism. That's partly because they're already suffering under a barrage of constant self-criticism, which the external criticism only reinforces, and partly because their overidentification, pathologizing, distrust of success, and other perfectionist characteristics make them vulnerable.

So, to be more resilient, work on overcoming your perfectionism.

Here are some other tips:

Share with care. While you want input from many sources, there is zero benefit to getting it from someone informationally, temperamentally, or otherwise unqualified to give it. So, share your work, thoughts, feelings, ideas, personal struggles, etc., only with those capable of offering a knowledgeable and compassionate response. This also applies to your family, by the way: they don't get a free pass to criticize you harshly, neglect you, marginalize you, etc.

Take the long view. Just as most "failures" turn out to be unimportant (Chapter 22), so, too, do most criticisms and rejections. Therefore, remind yourself, when you're hurting, that "this too shall pass."

Work to positively reframe your rejections. Here's a fun example from writer Chris Offutt:

> The notion of submitting anything to a magazine filled me with terror. A stranger would read my precious words, judge them deficient, and reject them, which meant I was worthless... My goal,

however, was not publication, which was still too scary a thought. My goal was a hundred rejections in a year.

I mailed my stories in multiple submissions and waited eagerly for their return, which they promptly did. Each rejection brought me that much closer to my goal—a cause for celebration, rather than depression. Eventually disaster struck. *The Coe Review* published my first story in spring 1990.[37]

Notice how empowering the positive reframing is, especially when combined with Offutt's playful approach. (Also, notice the overfocus on outcomes, overidentification, and other perfectionist characteristics that probably contributed to his being so scared of rejection to start with.)

Prioritize healing/cope lavishly. When you do experience a painful criticism or rejection, resist the temptation to minimize it or ignore your hurt. (In other words, ignore those who tell you to, "Get over it.") If you need to have a crying jag or a sulk—or a few—do that. But...

Don't isolate yourself. Sure, hide out for a little while if you want. But after that, discuss the situation with a friend, mentor, or therapist.

Speak truth to power, judiciously. Speaking truth to power can be a healing and empowering act that can also lead to changes that prevent others from being harmed the way you were. There's always a risk, however, that the person you're speaking to will respond negatively. So think carefully before doing it, perhaps asking yourself whether the offender is a good person who simply made a mistake, or someone who is often harsh or callous. The former may be worth having a discussion with, while the latter may not—and, if you're in doubt, it's probably best to err on the side of caution. (None of this is to say that you shouldn't let others know of the person's bad behavior, to the extent you feel safe doing so.) All of which brings us to the most important coping strategy of all...

Minimize the stuff you need to cope with. You do this by avoiding jobs, projects, and personal relationships with known harsh people, exploiters, and other problematic types. (Personally, I do my best to avoid even brief interactions with these kinds of people, as some can do an amazing amount of harm in a short time.) This rule is usually easy to follow, until it isn't. Sooner or later, you'll probably be tempted by, for instance:

A gig with someone with great skills and connections, but also a reputation for harshness.

A job at a prestigious company known for burning out its employees.

---

[37] Chris Offutt, "The Eleventh Draft." In Frank Conroy (ed.), *The Eleventh Draft*.

A romantic relationship with someone who is sexy and glamorous, but also self-centered. Or,

Some other opportunity that sets off your warning bells.

Just. Say. No. Relationships with toxic people and organizations rarely work out the way we hope they will, and frequently leave us worse off. (See, also, Chapter 44's discussion of how to decline unwanted commitments.)

Saying no to problematic projects and people isn't just a productivity strategy: it's a survival strategy and a profound form of self-care. But you can take things even further, not simply by avoiding the "bad" people and projects, but by actively searching out the "good" ones. Which brings us to...

Create an Empowered Career. Empowered careers are built on principles of kindness, compassion, cooperation, equality, transparency, non-exploitation, generosity (including forgiveness of honest mistakes), and a desire to succeed alongside others ("win/win"), rather than at their expense ("zero sum"). These are the kinds of careers that, along with being ethically desirable, can not only help you, and your colleagues and coworkers, succeed to the greatest extent possible, but have the most fun along the way. (Because you're working alongside the kindest, savviest, and most fun people.)

Of course, if you're working for an organization, you're subject to that organization's values and mores—and it's getting harder and harder to find organizations that treat workers well. Worker power roughly correlates with unionization, and unionization (in the United States at least) has been on a decline since the 1950s. Over the past few decades, workers have been working harder, and producing more, while receiving less. (Put another way, modern workers are keeping far less of the value they create than previous generations.) And I'm not just talking about salaries, either: organizations have been far less accommodating of their employees' basic human needs—e.g., for health care, a humane schedule that allows them time to take care of their personal and family needs, and a decent retirement. I wish I could say that it was just corporations that were exploitative, but you can find the same lack of basic consideration for workers even in government, education, health, and nonprofit work. (All fields where you'd expect organizations to treat their employees well.)

The tide is starting to turn, as union organizing (thankfully) is on the increase, but we've still got a long way to go.

Especially in an economy where many are devalued, prioritize working for the kindest, most humane, and most equitable organizations you can—

and within any organization, with the kindest, most humane, and most equitable people you can. ("Prioritize" means that other conditions, like salary and title, are secondary.) Always strive to work for effective organizations and teams that accomplish their goals, but not those that seek to do so through exploitation.

Be sure, also, to fully acquaint yourself with all of your employee benefits and rights. Employee benefits have declined alongside worker power, and so fewer workplaces offer perks like flextime, telecommuting, and tuition reimbursement. (Obviously, many people telecommuted during the COVID pandemic, but I'm talking about as a general trend.) Even when an employer does offer these kinds of benefits, however, some employees resist using them. Of course, there could be a valid reason for that, but sometimes the barrier is a lack of information or a reluctance to advocate for oneself. Once, in a time-management class, a woman who worked as a Boston public school teacher was bemoaning her long commute. "And you're not allowed to request a transfer to a school closer to where you live," she concluded, dismally.

"That's absolutely not true," said another student, who was sitting across from her at the table. "I'm a public school teacher and I got a transfer."

It was what we call a teachable moment.

Even if your workplace doesn't formally offer these benefits, it might not hurt to ask for them, assuming you have a good relationship with your supervisor. This is as good a time as any to mention that **sometimes we don't have enough faith in those around us**. I've worked with people who were absolutely convinced that they would receive no support from their family, friends, supervisor, coworkers, etc., on their time-management and other needs, only to discover that, once they finally asked, that support was readily offered. Often, people want to help us but don't know how until we ask. So ask!

Sometimes, the arrangement winds up being, "I'll give you time off now for your project if you work extra hours during our crunch season"—a nice win/win.

For entrepreneurs, the task is both easier and harder. Yes, you might have more choice as to whom you'll be working with. But many people who go into business thinking that it will free them from "having a boss" discover that having to answer to customers, suppliers, distributors, etc., is like having *many* bosses. (In general, you want to go into business for affirmative reasons, such as that you have a passion you want to share with the world, and not negative ones, like wanting to escape from the corporate world.)

Entrepreneurs in creative fields arguably have it toughest right now. Writers, musicians, artists, etc., have, for centuries, been at the mercy of capitalists, such as wealthy Renaissance patrons. These days, however, monopolistic corporations (as noted in Chapter 29) almost completely control access to audiences, thus throttling creative careers. Having a solid marketing and sales plan can help, but only so much. In this disempowering context, as in others, do your best to create a "pocket of empowerment" in which you can work and thrive. Many savvy writers have done well by turning to indie publishing, for instance, and many savvy musicians now seek to earn their living not from streaming, but live performances. These kinds of strategies aren't panaceas—far from it—but they can offer a more equitable arrangement than traditional business models that put you entirely at the mercy of large corporations.

36. Strategies for Difficult Conversations

I've been talking, mostly, about serious rejection and criticism, but what about the smaller offenses? You know: the comments and questions that may be a bit judgmental or callous, but are really mostly clueless. They're not the worst thing in the world but because our goal is to address, as much as possible, every obstacle to productivity, it's a good idea to learn how to recognize and be prepared for them.

Let's start with the **negative professional stereotypes**. Engineers are geeks (or nerds), writers and artists are impractical dreamers, government employees are slackers, and blue-collar workers are unintellectual. These kinds of inaccurate, and sometimes offensive, stereotypes get tiresome, especially after the hundredth or so time you've heard them.

Even the compliments can be problematic. Artists are told that they "must be creative," often with the implication that that's their defining, or only, virtue. Meanwhile, social workers and teachers are told that they "must be caring," often with gender stereotypes coming into play. The offenders can include your family, friends, acquaintances, and even strangers you meet at the laundromat or bus stop. In fact, you'll even hear these tired old stereotypes from people within your field. (Who really ought to know better.)

If you're on the receiving end of a tiresome comment, don't assume ill intent. (Especially if it's in the context of an otherwise supportive relationship.) The speaker is likely trying to make a connection, and maybe even trying to show respect. But they don't know how. If it's an occasional problem, it's probably best to ignore it. But if someone is frequently making the same tiresome comment, you should ask them to stop.

It's also helpful to compile a list of professional truths about your major and its practitioners. Far from being "nerds," for instance, many engineers tend to be technical, precise, skilled, playful, versatile, quantitative, curious, creative, clever, detailed-oriented, systems-oriented, analytical, innovative, and good with technology—and that's just for starters. Make it an expansive list! (It's not like every single engineer has to have every single one of those attributes. I'm generalizing.) This is a great exercise to do with friends in your field, and I actually wish universities would assign it as an exercise in their introductory courses for each major.

After you compile your list, review it every so often to neutralize the stereotypes and build pride in your field and yourself.

Then there are the **tricky inquiries**. I already discussed one type—the product-focused, "Is it finished yet? What's taking so long?"—in Chapter 31. But there are others. Writers, artists, and performers often get asked, for example, "Can you make any money doing that?"

Again, be nonperfectionist and don't assume ill intent. Also:

Remember the goal. It's not to convince the other person—you have no control over that—but to share as much of your truth as you want to share, in an empowered way.

Speak and act with confidence. Contrary to widespread belief, it hasn't actually been proven that acting confident can help you feel more confident. But if a confident voice and body language help you to feel better in the moment, then I would use those. A confident approach can also discourage others from persisting with an unwanted discussion. So practice saying your most uncomfortable answers—"Yes, I do make a part-time income from my art. It's not a big one, but that's not the primary goal."—in a confident voice, and also practice looking confident by making eye contact and smiling while you reply. (Acknowledging that this advice might be more difficult to follow for those who are neurodivergent, or whose cultures discourage eye contact.)

Educate instead of defending or justifying (as discussed in Chapter 31). Example: "I love writing romance because it's fun and many people enjoy it. Some readers have told me that my books have helped them get through a tough time, and I'm really happy about that."

Argue from authority (also discussed in Chapter 31). Example: "It typically takes a few years to break into the field. One of my mentors advised me to do some volunteer work with the national association to build my connections, and so that's what I'm doing."

Set boundaries. You do not have to answer every question put to you. So think about what you're comfortable sharing, and with whom, and practice gracefully pivoting away from unwanted requests for information. Example:

36. Strategies for Difficult Conversations

Questioner: Have you gotten an agent yet?
You: Nope, still looking! [Resists the temptation to offer further details.] How are things with you?
Questioner (persisting): It's pretty tough, eh?
You: Yes, but let's talk about something else, okay? How are the Phillies doing this year?

Boomerang the focus back on the listener. Example (if someone is grilling you about your music career): "So what kind of music do you like?"

Humor is a risky tactic because it's easy to screw up, and if you do screw it up, you risk sounding not just unfunny, but bitter or condescending. But give it a try, if you want. Example: "Why don't I get another job? Great idea! Maybe I'll stop by the job store on my way home and pick one up." By the way, professional comedians are able to get the jokes right because they spend lots of time practicing. Which brings us to...

Plan ahead and practice. Especially if you know a challenging encounter is coming up, plan out your answers to difficult questions and practice saying those answers with confidence. Each time you practice, you should hear yourself improve; and knowing that you've practiced will, in itself, boost your confidence.

Make sure you're comfortable with your own values and choices. Remember Chapter 24's point about how we're often ambivalent because we at least partly share the other person's view? If you truly think that a humbler lifestyle is a good trade-off for getting to do work that you love and feel is important, then it shouldn't bother you too much if others disagree. Yes, it's tedious if they keep harping on it, and you should definitely ask them to stop. But the occasional ill-chosen comment in an otherwise caring relationship can be forgiven and forgotten. And finally,

Create your own "family." Meaning, a group of loving people who share your values and can provide support, perhaps in ways your family of origin can't. You can find these people online, of course, but it's best to have at least a small supportive community in real life.

The ability to respond to even challenging inquiries with ease and confidence is a great skill to have and a sign of some excellent empowerment. This is another category of behavior that is best learned by watching experienced, nonperfectionist mentors, so that's yet another reason to seek some out.

When You're the Critic

I hope the last couple of chapters will help you better understand, and cope with, any criticisms and rejections you may have received, or might receive in the future. I also hope they inspire you to be a kind and competent critic (and "rejector") yourself. You achieve that by doing pretty much the opposite of everything I've been discussing—i.e., delivering your criticisms as kindly, fairly, privately, etc., as possible—and by not criticizing too much. Criticism is a very strong spice, and so in most cases just a pinch or two is fine—and only after getting the person's explicit or implicit permission for such feedback. ("Implicit" permission, by the way, is what we give teachers, mentors, editors, and others with a professional mandate to critique our work.) Also:

Always follow through when you offer to critique someone's work, and do so in a timely way. If you don't, it can not only inconvenience, but hurt, the person who trusted you. This means, obviously, that you should think carefully before agreeing to critique someone's work, especially if it is outside your specialty. I've gotten stuck a few times by agreeing to critique someone's work, only to realize, later on, that I really wasn't the right person to do so. The ensuing conversations were, to say the least, awkward. (An exception would be if they want your opinion as a non-specialist in their field.)

Always find something good to say. If you don't like the work itself, then find something to praise in the person's process or approach. (As discussed in Chapter 14, praising their process is a good idea in any case.)

Get specific. As Joni B. Cole writes in her book *Toxic Feedback*, "Writers…can handle specifics. It's the generalities that bring them to their knees. 'Your story didn't work for me.' 'I don't get it.' 'This isn't my thing.' Those [...] only serve to leave writers feeling more at a loss than usual."

Be generous. You don't have to write (or speak) pages, but going into detail about two or three specific points will be helpful, and also show that you care.

Ask what kind of feedback is desired. Example: "I'd be happy to read your essay [or, look at your painting, or listen to your song], but can you give me some idea of what kind of feedback you'd like?"

Use the "sandwich" technique: put a criticism in between two compliments. It's kind of obvious but still helps.

Critique the project on its own terms, instead of comparing it to the project you would have done. Granted, this can be difficult—and if you sense that it's going to be *really* difficult, then you should probably decline the request to critique.

Especially if you've got some strong criticisms to convey, do your best to **communicate either in person or via phone or videocall.** Email and texting don't allow for much emotion and nuance.

Everyone should learn how to deliver constructive criticism, especially if they desire to mentor or teach others. And it goes without saying (or should) that you should also be an effective *receiver* of constructive criticism. Don't be one of those people who gets defensive or angry when someone is legitimately trying to help. (Especially if you asked for that help.)

Exercise 18

Can you think of any times when you criticized or rejected someone in a needlessly hurtful way? What could you have done differently, and what will you do differently in the future? (It may not be too late to apologize and make amends.)

37. How to Stay Safe (and Productive) on Social Media

Social media is one of those activities, like parenting or managing a chronic health issue, whose very ubiquity can cause us to discount its challenges. But just because "everyone is doing it," doesn't mean it's easy to do, especially in a safe and productive way.

Although the various social media platforms are amazing, game-changing, society-evolving technologies, they are also cauldrons of abuse and dysfunction where you'll find every single perfectionist characteristic discussed in Part II, and every form of criticism and rejection discussed in this section, in abundance. So it's no surprise that, as discussed in Chapter 17, social media use has been linked to depression and anxiety in students and others.

Of course, you'll also find rampant sexism, racism, religious bias, homophobia, transphobia, ableism, classism, and nativism online.

Then there's the whole set of *other* problems intrinsic to social media, including reductiveness (from the often terse communications); a lack of body language, vocal tone, and other cues; a lack of privacy; a lack of boundaries (so that your family and supervisor can read stuff you'd normally just show your friends); and the pressure to post frequently. Plus, all the usual creative quandaries. As renowned blogger Jason Kottke put it:

> Doing kottke.org is this constant battle with myself: staying in my comfort zone vs. finding opportunities for growth, posting what I like or find interesting vs. attempting to suss out what "the reader" might want, celebrating the popular vs. highlighting the obscure, balancing the desire to define what it is I do here vs. appreciating that no one really knows (myself included), posting clickable things

vs. important things I know will be unpopular, protecting myself against criticism vs. accepting it as a gift, deciding when to provoke & challenge vs. when to comfort & entertain, feeling like this is frivolous vs. knowing this site is important to me & others, being right vs. accepting I'll make mistakes, and saying something vs. letting the content and its creators speak for themselves.[38]

Kottke has been blogging for more than twenty years and is considered a master at it: if he still finds it challenging, I guess we can all be forgiven for feeling the same way. In any case, you probably do want and need to be on social media, at least to some degree, especially if you're in a creative or entrepreneurial field. Also, we—meaning society—need you to be on social media, to the extent that you're comfortable. We need as many voices and visions as possible, and your voice is especially important if you're a member of a marginalized or otherwise oppressed community. With all that in mind, here are some steps you can take to stay safe (and productive) on social media, and maybe even have some fun:

Prioritize safety. Don't pressure yourself to participate more than you'd like, or in ways you don't like, and don't let anyone else pressure you either.

Work on your nonperfectionism. Remember: it's the foundation of resilience.

Be strategic. Figure out your goal(s) for participation and tailor your online presence accordingly. If your primary goal is to communicate with family and friends, for instance, then tighten up your privacy settings. If it's to advance your career, keep things professional. If it's to promote a political viewpoint, you might want to engage more broadly—but still, not with everyone.

Consider having two accounts. A private one just for close friends, and a public one for everyone else. That way, you have at least one account where you don't feel the need to censor yourself.

Find role models whose online success you'd like to emulate. Look for those who are relatable—i.e., ordinary people, not celebrities—and two to ten years further along the path than you.

Block the troublemakers. If someone is causing you stress or pain, block them, even if they happen to be related to you. Do it sooner rather than later.

---

[38] https://kottke.org/20/07/a-moment-of-reflection-on-the-paradox-of-individual-creative-work

Don't feed the trolls! If someone is playing devil's advocate, or sealioning, or being a "reply guy," or otherwise posting in bad faith, don't feel obligated to respond.[39] You don't owe them your time and attention. (Politician Alexandria Ocasio-Cortez wisely compared one right-winger's incessant demands that she debate him to street harassment.[40]) Ignore them, and they'll probably get bored and go away.

Trust your gut. If you're not mostly enjoying your time spent on social media, something's wrong.

If you're being harassed, stalked, or threatened, get help *immediately*. Keep records of all incidents, including not just a timeline, but printouts of messages, texts, posts, etc. https://www.fightcyberstalking.org offers downloadable forms for recording incidents, and also information for dealing with harassers on different platforms. Other useful resources include: http://www.cyberbullying.org/resources/, http://1800victims.org/crime-type/cybercrimes/, , and http://www.gameshotline.org harassment on gaming platforms or in gaming communities).

For Those Posting Political Content

A few more steps, specifically for those posting political or otherwise controversial content:

Know what you're doing. Community organizing and persuasion are skills, and if you "wing it" your efforts may backfire. More generally, you always want to work strategically, avoiding what famed animal activist Henry Spira called "hyperactivism," which is when someone works hard, but without a strategy, so that they're not achieving much for their efforts.[41] It seems a particular risk online, where so many activists get sucked into endless, unproductive arguments, either with those on their side or the opposition. (Whenever I see an activist arguing with someone intransigent who also has very few followers, I wonder what they think they're accomplishing.)

Filter your inputs. Many well-meaning activists post endless streams of relentlessly negative and disturbing content about world problems. Yes, they mean well, and yes, you need to stay informed—but please ask yourself

---

[39] Citations for this sentence:
https://www.reddit.com/r/Feminism/comments/dry3dn/let_me_play_devils_advocate/ (devil's advocate), https://en.wikipedia.org/wiki/Sealioning (sealioning), https://twitter.com/i/events/1041376202391343104?lang=en (reply guy), https://meta.wikimedia.org/wiki/What_is_a_troll (bad faith).
[40] https://twitter.com/aoc/status/1027729430137827328
[41] www.satyamag.com/june96/spira.html

what is accomplished by continuously exposing yourself to the same (often disturbingly graphical) content? As a psychologist and activist I once knew said of this problem, "You accomplish nothing by constantly retraumatizing yourself." So, maybe limit yourself to following a few high-quality accounts, while blocking or muting most others.

Expect pushback. Remember that your goal is to (choose one or all): shake up the status quo, speak truth to power (or take that power down!), "Comfort the afflicted and afflict the comfortable," in the words of journalist Finley Peter Dunne, and/or, "Go where you are least wanted, because that is where you are most needed," as per abolitionist Abigail Kelley Foster. You obviously can't do those things without making at least some people mad, so be prepared for pushback and learn to see it as a sign you're having an impact.

Remember your silent audience. Even if some people are responding negatively or obnoxiously to your posts, there are probably others—and, perhaps, many more—who are quietly appreciating them (and see the obnoxious bullies for who they are).

Support others. If you see someone being picked on online, support them with a public comment or private message.

Educate yourself on your online rights, and use technologies appropriate to your values and situation. These sites will help: https://www.eff.org/pages/tools/, https://www.fsf.org, https://www.aclu.org/issues/privacy-technology#current, and https://electronicintifada.net/content/guide-online-security-activists/17536.

One of the major problems with social media is that it can eat up so much of our time. If only there were a tool that could help us keep everything in balance... Oh wait—there is! It's called "time management" and I discuss it in the next section. See you there!

Part V

Abundance

38. An Awesome Liberation

The big reason to practice time management is that **there's no such thing as unmanaged time.** If you're not managing your time, someone else is managing it for you. That could be your family, friends, employer, colleagues, coworkers, or classmates. Or it could be corporations trying to sell you a particular product or lifestyle. Bad enough to let those who truly care about you rule your time—but corporations?

The capitalist / consumerist lifestyle common in the U.S. and some other countries emphasizes long workdays (often with additional long commutes), with much of the rest of your time spent on chores. "Free time," after all those obligations, is often limited to television, Web surfing, gaming, and other passive and/or isolating activities, both because those are the easiest options available and because you're too tired to do anything else. Meanwhile, relationships, socializing, self-care, caregiving, and community work—all the major contributors to a happy and healthy life and society, in other words—are given short shrift.[42] Is it any wonder that, in such societies, so many are stressed, unhealthy, and unhappy? That there are so many troubled relationships? And so many unraveling communities?

---

[42] Notice how many of the countries that provide workers with the most paid time off (https://en.wikipedia.org/wiki/List_of_minimum_annual_leave_by_country) also top the World Happiness Report's list of happiest countries (https://en.wikipedia.org/wiki/World_Happiness_Report#2019_report). Also note that many of those same countries also provide strong health, housing, and educational benefits, thus further improving individuals' lives while simultaneously freeing their time by easing their caregiving and other obligations.

Our time use is also hugely gendered, with women almost always on the losing end of the equation. Globally, we women remain hugely disproportionately responsible not just for caregiving for children and others, but for household chores and maintenance work. At the same time, far less of our labor is paid than men's.[43] Furthermore, women are still frequently encouraged to stay quiet and subjugate their needs to those of others, and so overgiving (Chapter 45) remains a problem.

I teach—and, in this book, will be discussing—what I call **Values-Based Time Management (VBTM)**. Unlike some other time-management systems that focus narrowly on maximizing your work output, VBTM's goal is more holistic: to help you to align, as much as possible, your actions with your values. VBTM also concerns itself with both your professional and personal lives. That's not just because it doesn't make sense to only manage half your time, but because your personal life is important.

Like most time-management systems, VBTM involves budgeting, scheduling, and tracking your time, all of which I'll be discussing. But the core is identifying, and then relentlessly prioritizing, the activities that are truly important to you.

VBTM, in other words, maximizes the chances that you'll achieve a happy, healthy, and productive life—however *you* define that. And here are some other reasons to do it:

Success makes you busier. (As discussed in Chapter 23.) Developing a time-management practice today will help you to cope with the flood of opportunities we're all hoping you'll be deluged with tomorrow. This also applies to your personal life, by the way. Many people aspire to not just a great career, but a great family life, a comfortable home, and to do good work in their community. Despite perfectionist media that implies that such a life is easily attainable, it's actually a lot to handle. But time management can help.

Society promotes unhealthy ideas of time use. Many people still believe, for instance, that the busier you are, the more successful and/or important you must be. Or that multitasking is a good idea. (Chapter 5 debunked that one.) Or that they work best under pressure. Speaking of which...

No one works best under pressure. And those who say they do are deluding themselves. Sure, pressure may terrorize you into finally overcoming your procrastination and focusing on your work. But there's no way that

---

[43] See, for example: https://www.bls.gov/news.release/atus.nr0.html down to the discussion of childcare.) And
https://unstats.un.org/unsd/gender/chapter4/chapter4.html

38. An Awesome Liberation

that work will ever equal the quantity or quality of work done under conditions of abundant time and attention, such as time management can provide. Besides, as discussed earlier, using pressure and other punishments as motivators will only make it harder for you to do your work in the future.

Last but not least...

You'll attract the best people. "Game recognizes game," as they say—and good time managers want to work with other good time managers, partly because they know that doing so will boost their own productivity, and partly because they know that the converse also applies: working with someone who doesn't manage their time well will drag them down. (Through their lack of reliability, missed deadlines, etc.)

Good time managers also want to have personal relationships with other good time managers for the same reasons.

Here's the good news: **for all its liberating potential, time management often comes down to making just a few simple changes in your life and habits.** That will become clear as Chapters 39 through 45 continue to explore the fundamental ideas underlying VBTM. Then, Chapters 46 and 47 will tell you how to use those ideas to create the values-driven time budget and schedule that work best for you, and also how to follow through on living that schedule.

39. What Makes a Good Time Manager

A **Good Time Manager (GTM)** makes time management a priority, which means that they not only do their time budgeting and scheduling and tracking (Chapters 46 and 47), but are also **optimizers**. They're always asking themselves questions like, "Did I do this task as efficiently as I could have?", "Was this event a good use of my time?", and "Is this [personal or professional] relationship working for me?" (And acting on the answers.) Please note that this inner Q&A is *always* supportive and encouraging, and *never* perfectionistically harsh. Always be your own best coach.

Implicit in being a time optimizer is that **you value small increments of time**, both for their own sake and because they add up. Reclaim just fifteen minutes of underutilized time a day and you'll gain more than ninety hours—the equivalent of more than two work weeks!—a year.

Now, a lot of people think they already understand all this. They go around saying stuff like, "Time is money." But watch them and you'll see them squander their precious time in ways they never would their cash. Also, they're wrong, because time actually happens to be far more valuable than money. That's not just because it's finite, with even the richest person being limited to 24 hours a day; it's also because time can create outcomes that money can't, and those happen to be the most valuable outcomes.

Consider two students. One attends an expensive college, and also buys the best computer, textbooks, etc., but rarely does their work. The other attends a cheaper school and makes do with cheaper supplies, but is diligent. Who will get educated?

Or, think of two people trying to get fit. One spends thousands on a gym membership and fancy workout clothes but never uses them. The other

39. What Makes a Good Time Manager

spends $100 on a decent pair of running shoes and some used weights, then runs or works out most days. Who will get fit?

Finally, think of two parents. One is always buying expensive gifts for their kids but rarely spends any time with them. The other doesn't have a lot of money to spend but tries their best to be present. Who will have the better relationship?

You get the idea—and it's not a new one. Around 2,000 years ago, the Stoic philosopher Seneca, in his powerful essay "On the Shortness of Life," said of those who misuse their time: "They are trifling with life's most precious commodity, being deceived because it is an intangible thing, not open to inspection and therefore reckoned very cheap."

Professionally and personally, GTMs are busy but not frantic. They meet their deadlines and do quality work. They show up on time, or a bit early, and prepared. They also prioritize sleep, nutrition, exercise, and other self-care. All of this means that they're as productive, healthy, and happy as possible, given their circumstances, and that they're not just great team members, but natural leaders and mentors. And so, interesting people and opportunities are always coming their way.

One of the best things about being a GTM is that you can accommodate the occasional interruption. If you encounter someone who needs assistance, for instance, you can offer it without derailing your entire day. (See below.) Ditto for a small fun interruption, like a coworker's birthday party at work.

Are GTMs like this 100% of the time? Of course not: they have their "off" days like everyone else, and sometimes their "off" weeks, months, or even years. (And expecting someone to be doing well at anything "100% of the time" is perfectionist.) But even during difficult times, a GTM will function better than they would have without their time management skills, and those skills will also help them to get back on track as quickly as possible.

Unfortunately, judging by the frequent news stories about workaholism, "time poverty," and similar problems, there aren't a lot of GTMs out there. Most people, in fact, are probably **Poor Time Managers (PTMs)** who constantly overcommit themselves. As a result, they're frequently late, missing deadlines, and handing in poor-quality work. Also, most PTMs aren't exactly a picture of health and happiness. Mostly, they're walking around stressed, ill, fatigued, and depleted.

Needless to say, a PTM isn't anyone's idea of a good team member, much less a leader. Professionally and personally, GTMs tend to avoid relationships with PTMs, whose chronic unreliability not only creates a huge strain, but greatly lessens the chances of a successful outcome.

Unsurprisingly, there's a perfectionist angle to all this. Both overscheduling and expecting yourself to function without adequate self-care are classic grandiose behaviors. (See Chapter 13.)

PTMs aren't the worst-off people, however: those would be the **Wannabe Time Managers (WTMs)**. They're dabblers, trying a little time management here and there, but they won't commit. As a result, they often wind up experiencing all the inconveniences of the practice while getting few or none of the benefits. They also tend to be deluded about how much time management they're actually doing. Many think that they are "almost a GTM" or "halfway between a GTM and PTM." In reality, however, most are far closer to PTMs than GTMs. (From now on, whenever I mention PTMs, you can assume I also mean WTMs.)

Why Being Busy Isn't the Virtue Many People Think It Is

The signature behavior of PTMs is rushing around. People in time-dysfunctional cultures tend to see rushing as a sign of ambition or importance. ("Sorry! Gotta run! Three meetings this afternoon!") But rushing is horrible. We've already seen, in Chapter 26, how it impairs our ability to learn and grow. But that's just one of the problems it causes. Rushing also impairs us physically and emotionally (all those stress hormones), intellectually (see Chapter 42's discussion of cognitive capacity), and even relationally (we treat both loved ones and strangers worse when we're in a rush).

Rushing even impairs our ethical functioning. This was demonstrated in a classic social psychology experiment by John M. Darley and C. Daniel Batson,[44] in which forty Princeton seminarians were asked to write, and then later record, a sermon. Each was assigned one of two topics to write about: either, (a) the ethically instructive parable of the Good Samaritan, in which, as you may recall, a king and a priest pass by a wounded man without stopping to help, but a "humble Samaritan" does the right thing and stops; or (b) the more ethically neutral topic of career paths for seminarians. After each seminarian had written his (they were all male) sermon, he was then given one of three instructions:
- He had plenty of time to get over to the recording studio (which was located in another building).
- He was on time, but shouldn't dawdle. Or,

---

[44] John M. Darley and C. Daniel Batson, "'From Jerusalem to Jericho': A study of situational and dispositional variables in helping behavior." In Elliot Aronson (ed.), *Readings About the Social Animal*, 7th Ed.

- He was late! The recording staff was waiting for him and he had to get to the studio right now!

Here's the twist: each seminarian, while en route to the studio, encountered a man lying in the street, seemingly ill and in distress. (He was actually an actor hired by the experimenters.) In other words, the seminarian was presented with the Good Samaritan scenario in real life!

What would he do? (What would YOU do?)

Not to leave you in suspense: the experimenters found that the seminarians in the third group, who were rushing to get to the studio, were far less likely to stop and help than the others—*and this was true even for those who had just written an entire sermon on the Good Samaritan*. All that thought and analysis—not to mention the basic helping orientation of most seminarians—flew right out the window just because they were rushed.

Darley and Batson concluded that, "Ethics becomes a luxury as the speed of our daily lives increases." They also urged us not to be too hard on the "non-helpers," who, they said, were caught in a conflict between their obligation to help the needy person and their obligation to the experimenters.

The bottom line is that, **when you're rushing, you're not the person you're capable of being: not physically, intellectually, emotionally, relationally, or ethically. Moment by moment, you're only living up to a part of your potential.**

The opposite of rushing could be defined as presence, mindfulness, or the ability to "be here now," as Ram Dass famously put it. Also, the ability to devote abundant—or, as abundant as possible—time, energy, and attention to the people and things that are truly important to you. Values-Based Time Management will help you locate and focus on all those priorities so that you can live a life filled not just with accomplishment but interest, meaning, love, and joy.

Exercise 19

Journal about how much rushing you do every day, how that rushing affects your work and life, and how things might improve if you could stop rushing.

40. Investing Your Time

When I said, in the last chapter, that time is more valuable than money, I wasn't saying that money is unimportant. Of course it's important—and you should definitely take the time to learn some money management. But research has shown that, after our basic material needs are met, the yields of time, including good health, good relationships, and a sense of personal fulfillment, become primary.[45] Also, people who value time over money tend to be happier in general.[46]

Time does have something important in common with money, however: you can invest it. You're probably familiar with financial investments, like stocks or real estate, that increase in value over time, thus earning you a "return." Buy $100 worth of stocks today and, if you've chosen well, you can sell them later for $200. (Or, sometimes, way more.) Personal financial experts tell us that anything that's not an investment is an expense, including not just your latest impulse purchase, but essentials like food, transportation, and clothing. All expenses, including the essential ones, lose value over time. (You can't resell that bag of groceries you just bought, or last month's train pass.) Experts therefore advise us to minimize even our essential expenses so that we can put as much money as possible into investments.

Time investments work pretty much the same way—except that, as discussed, a time investment can yield not just money, but health, happiness, love, and even more time. So, as important as investing your money is, it's

---

[45] See, for instance, http://www.pewsocialtrends.org/2008/04/30/who-wants-to-be-rich/ Notice how, in the study, the most valued priority across all demographics, by a wide margin, is, "to have enough free time."
[46] https://www.nytimes.com/2016/09/11/opinion/sunday/what-should-you-choose-time-or-money.html

even more important to invest your time. The major categories of time investments are:

Self-care, including good nutrition, exercise, sleep, grooming, medical and therapy appointments and, for some, a meditation or spiritual practice. Poor Time Managers (PTMs) often stint on this and wind up going through their days exhausted and depleted. Good Time Managers (GTMs), in contrast, aim for abundant self-care, and also understand that **the more ambitious your goals, or the tougher the barriers you face, the more self-care you need.**

Some activists and other good people mistakenly believe that self-care is an indulgence in a world beset with many urgent problems. But skimping on it makes you less effective and is also likely to lead to burnout. As the poet/activist Audre Lorde famously said, "Caring for myself is not self-indulgence, it is self-preservation, and that is an act of political warfare."

Relationships. You know: that thing that many people, at the end of their life, wish they had devoted more time to.

Values-driven work, meaning work you do for love and not just a paycheck. (I frequently refer to this category as your "vocation" or "mission.") Some caregiving, creative, spiritual, and other practices would also belong in this category.

Education, by which I mean both the formal pursuit of a degree, and the less-formal but equally serious and important lifelong education that you participate in after your college years. Some people continue to accrue degrees and certifications throughout their lives, while others skip the degrees but take whatever online or offline courses happen to strike their fancy, while still others do a lot of independent reading and study. It's all good. The important thing is that you keep on learning and growing.

Replenishing recreation. Activities that are fun and relaxing, and that also leave you healthier and happier (a.k.a., "replenished"). They tend to be active and engaging, and they also tend to connect you with others and/or nature and/or certain aspects of yourself, like your creativity, intellect, athleticism, or senses. Examples include socializing, sports, an art or craft, outdoor activities, and travel.

Activism / Community Organizing. This is perhaps the highest yielding of all the investment categories. Don't believe me? Many of us have benefited from opportunities that wouldn't have been possible even a couple of generations ago unless you happened to have been born rich, white, straight, non-disabled, and male. Generations of activists and community organizers fighting for social justice on all fronts, including labor, education, race, gender, and disability, have granted us all some precious opportunities—which, let's not forget, are still beyond the reach of many. So, pay it forward by investing a few hours a month on whichever social justice cause speaks most to your heart. Along with the good you'll be doing, you'll also find that activism yields some terrific personal benefits, including the opportunity to do meaningful work alongside some of the best people you'll ever meet.

For more on activism, see my book *The Lifelong Activist*—and please note that I'm talking about activism / community organizing and not volunteer work. Volunteering is good, but activism is better because it seeks to remedy the conditions, such as poverty, that make the volunteering necessary to start with.

The final category of time investment is one that many forget, but it's actually the most important one because it underpins the success of all the rest:

Planning and Management. Success doesn't just happen: you have to plan for it and then manage the process as it unfolds. You should, in fact, plan and manage all of the above investment categories, including those we typically don't think of as requiring planning and management, such as relationships. (Many people wing it in this crucial area and then wind up with a failed marriage or alienated kids.) You should also plan and manage your resources, including your information, money, property, and (hello) time. All this planning and management may sound like a lot of work but it really isn't, since a little goes a long way. Planning for a successful romantic relationship, for instance, might involve reading a few books on relationships, working with a therapist to overcome any relevant barriers, and then developing a set of principles (e.g., mutual support and open communication) and habits (e.g., weekly date nights and prompt resolution of conflicts) that you and your partner agree to moving forward. Career planning might involve more initial work but the effort still remains small compared with the potential yield of a satisfying decades-long career.

Assuming you're not in the midst of actively planning your career or some other major life goal, two hours per week should be fine for all your planning and management activities.

Generally speaking, you want to put some time into each of your investment categories every week. Obviously, some weeks are busier than others and you might need to put off doing your activism or planning (say) during exceptionally busy times. But you shouldn't do that for long periods.

Also, please note that sometimes an activity fulfills two categories (e.g., socializing counts as both relationships and recreation), and sometimes one category is subsumed into another, e.g., you can be educating yourself as part of your vocation and planning.

So those are the time investments. All other activities are **time expenses,** including:

Chores, including housekeeping, errands, etc.

A "**day job**" you're doing just, or mostly, for money.

Your **commute**, an often time-consuming activity that is also often very stressful. Pre-COVID, when many people started telecommuting, the average U.S. commute (round-trip) was 52 minutes/day.[47] However, a PTM's commute is likely to be longer than average. (And I expect that we'll return to long commutes soon.)

Escapist recreation. In contrast to replenishing recreation, escapist activities tend to be sedentary, isolating, and disconnecting. Television is the obvious example, but social media and gaming can also qualify, despite their superficial social aspects. Acknowledging that while, in some cases, these media and apps can be fabulous, and also that some groups (e.g., people with disabilities) rely on them, generally speaking, you want to limit your use.

Procrastination is also a time expense. It may seem funny to think of it that way since none of us really wants to procrastinate. But when you think about it, that's true of all the other expenses, too. (Except, perhaps, for the escapism.)

The final category of time expense is: any activity you're doing just to kill time—and what a horrible expression that is—or out of habit, or because of convention, or because of a reluctance to say no (see Chapters 44 and 45).

The line between time investments and expenses isn't hard and fast: an activity can be either, depending on who's doing it and why. **If you really enjoy something, and feel it enhances your life, then it's an investment.** But if someone else finds it a tedious chore, then it's an expense for them.

It's also possible to overdo an investment, in which case it becomes an expense. We already know what that's called: Quasiproductive Procrastination (Chapter 5).

---

[47] https://www.census.gov/library/visualizations/interactive/travel-time.html

41. Shifting from Expenses to Investments

Similar to money management, a major goal of time management is to shift as much of your time as you can out of expenses and into investments. Doing this is arguably even more important for your time than your money because everything we purchase winds up costing us twice, time-wise: once in the time it takes to earn the money to purchase it, and forever after in the time it takes to maintain it. "The things we own, own us," as the saying goes. (And, obviously, buying a lot of stuff is also not good for the environment.)

An investment-centered life offers some outstanding yields, including not just increased productivity and achievement, but more health, happiness, fulfillment, and joy. You do the shift from expenses to investments systematically via budgeting, which I discuss in Chapter 46. But why not get started now? Here are a few suggestions for reducing expenses that you might want to implement immediately:

- Quit (responsibly—don't leave anyone in the lurch) any committees, groups, or other activities that you aren't enjoying or that aren't accomplishing much.
- Quit (but not callously) any relationships that aren't working for you (for example, people you're seeing mainly out of habit or obligation).
- Work double shifts at your job to lower your commuting and preparation time.
- Set a time limit for household chores—say, half an hour of cleaning per room per week. (Without a limit, they have a way of "expanding" to fill all your available time.) If you live with others, make sure that everyone is doing their fair share.

- Buddy up with a housemate or friend for chores, so that, for instance, you do all the laundry or grocery shopping one week, and they do it all the next.
- Invest in great tools that make chores easier and quicker (e.g., great house cleaning supplies).
- Decline and delegate wherever possible. (See Chapter 44.)

A lot of these steps involve eliminating, or at least cutting down on, stuff you don't want to be doing anyway. In theory, that should be a no-brainer, but perfectionism, guilt, obligation, convention, peer pressure, and an overgiving habit (Chapter 45) can all get in the way. Be compassionate and patient with yourself while working to overcome these barriers, but definitely do work to overcome them.

As you eliminate expenses, start filling the liberated time with investments. Your choices will be based on your own particular values and goals, but a good rule of thumb is to put two-thirds of your liberated time into your vocation and one-third into self-care and replenishing recreation. (Alternatively, for those with significant parenting or other caregiving needs: one-third into vocation, one-third into parenting / caregiving, and one-third into self-care.) Doing that should lead to a relatively quick improvement in both your productivity and your quality of life.

Reining in Your Escapist Activities

Probably the hardest expenses for many people to cut or trim are their escapist ones, such as social media, gaming, and television. Acknowledging that these can sometimes be stress-relieving—and essential for some, including those who are disabled—they nevertheless have significant drawbacks, including that they're typically very sedentary and isolating. They also often promote terrible values: see, for instance, social media's ubiquitous perfectionism and some gaming communities' misogyny. Even when one of these activities has a social component, the socializing is often shallow or what psychologists call *parasocial*, which means that it is one-sided and unreciprocated. Psychologists have expressed many concerns about parasocial relationships, including that they reinforce unrealistic relationship models, erode people's ability to socialize in real life, and can render people vulnerable to advertising and other influences.[48]

---

[48] https://www.pbs.org/wgbh/nova/article/parasocial-relationships/

In Chapter 46's sample budget I allocate 1.5 hours a day for escapist activities. That's actually a huge chunk of your precious time—around 10% of your waking hours—but it isn't so huge that it's likely to sabotage your success. Still, if you're happy doing less, that's terrific. (Psychologist Melissa G. Hunt, whose research on social media harms I cited earlier, recommends limiting your social media use to thirty minutes a day.) As with all Values-Based Time Management, the important thing is to be honest about your needs and preferences.

For those interested in reducing the amount of escapism they do, here are some suggestions:

- Disconnect part-time, as discussed in Chapter 6.
- Use clocks. Remember, from Chapter 6, how removing clocks from your workspace can help you work longer? The obverse is also true: if you display a clock prominently while gaming or doing some other escapist activity, that can encourage you to limit that activity. It's best if the clock is either analog[49] or, if digital, a separate device from your phone or PC. (Like the kitchen timer you're using for your Timed Work Intervals.)
- Use timers, as Gregory Ferenstein (Chapter 6) did. These can help to interrupt the trancelike ludic loop so you can change to a healthier activity. Again, it's better to use either an analog timer or a standalone digital one.
- Have some low-stress and easy forms of replenishing recreation readily available. It could be some light, fun reading, or a fun hobby like sketching, knitting, baking, beading, or gardening.
- Be mindful of the opportunity costs, meaning the more rewarding activities you could be doing if you weren't putting so much time into escapism. (Try not to be one of those people who complains online about all the cool stuff they could be doing if they weren't online so much.)
- Slow down / stop rushing. As noted in Chapter 39, rushing is highly stressful, and the stress often increases our need for escapism. (As you empty your schedule of unnecessary tasks and commitments, this should happen automatically—assuming, of course, that you are vigilant about not replacing them with new ones.)
- Be mindful of apps' negative aspects. I personally find social media engrossing, entertaining, and informative—but also, often, tedious, repetitive, shallow, stressful, and banal. Staying mindful of these kinds

---

[49] https://www.sciencedirect.com/science/article/pii/S2352853215000140

of downsides can make it easier for you to resist the temptation to overindulge.
- Be mindful of apps' political and social context. Fun as apps, games, videos, television shows, and other distractions are, they were created by corporations specifically to hijack and monetize your time and personal data. Many of the platforms have obvious and well-publicized problems, including privacy violations and an unwillingness to deal with racist, sexist, and otherwise harmful content. Staying mindful of these kinds of political and social concerns, along with those pertaining to your own personal welfare, can help you resist the temptation to overindulge.

So far, I've been talking mostly about small and incremental changes. But there's one major change you can make that, all by itself, can help you shift a lot of your time into investments. It's called frugality and I discuss it below.

Getting Frugal

Let's get one potential confusion out of the way immediately: **frugality isn't deprivation, it's intentionality.** Whether you think of your frugality as "living simply" or "minimalism" or "living below my means" or simply "being frugal," it all comes down to buying only what you truly need and want, and not what you don't: for example, the excellent wardrobe, cookware, art supplies, and/or vacations that truly enhance your life, but not the fancy car, furniture, gym membership, and/or electronics that don't. Again, these are just examples: you should make your choices based on your own values and goals—although a new car is literally *the* textbook financial expense, with most cars losing about 25% of their resale value the minute you drive them off the dealer's lot.

Frugality is, of course, a necessity in tough economies where wages are depressed, but it's a wise choice even in better economies. And while many people are frugal out of necessity, I'm also talking about being frugal when you do have some discretionary funds. This kind of "optional frugality" can be powerfully liberating, freeing you to be able to, for instance:
- Work at a job or career you truly want, even if it doesn't pay as well as some others.
- Work part time while also pursuing a cherished but low-paid or unpaid arts, activist, travel, caregiving, or other mission.

- Live in the community you really want to live in (because it's safer, more fun, less of a commute, etc.) instead of having to live where it's cheapest.

Frugality can also, obviously, help you to save money, and that, in turn, can help you achieve costly goals such as home ownership, parenthood, business ownership, and retirement.

So let's get frugal! It's good to pinch pennies where you can, but a Good Time Manager (GTM) will take this liberating step to the max using two techniques. The first is **living small**, by which I mean either living in a small space (thus reducing rent, utilities, furniture, cleaning, and other expenses), or sharing your big space with others. This can seem like a bold move if everyone around you is equating success with constantly moving into larger and fancier spaces. But it can really pay off in terms of freeing your time, money, and attention for the things you truly love.

True, it can be hard to find good housemates (if you're opting for that choice). But it helps if you are clear about your needs and desires. I once found two great housemates by posting an ad that included language like this: "Seeking housemates for a three-person household where we don't eat together every day because we're all busy and focused on our projects...a good apartment for someone who wants a quiet and companionable living situation where you have a lot of privacy and personal space." Since all the other posts were for households with lots of communal meals and other socializing, I worried that my ad sounded unfriendly. But it got me two housemates who were a perfect fit.

The other excellent frugality technique is **thrifting**. Find a good thrift store, resale shop, or consignment shop—meaning one in or near an affluent neighborhood, and that's also spacious, well-lit, and well-organized—and make a point of stopping by once or twice a month. Make a note of which days they put out new merchandise, and befriend the staff, who will sometimes let you know when a good shipment, or an item you need, has come in. Over time, you can acquire a great wardrobe (including jewelry and other accessories), or great kitchenware, sports gear, furniture, decorative pieces, etc., for pennies on the dollar.

Obviously, you can thrift online, too—and many do that with gusto. But it can be hard for even well-meaning and honest vendors to describe a used item accurately, and the shipping costs can also be prohibitive. So try to find at least one local store.

41. Shifting from Expenses to Investments

Although there are plenty of books, blogs, and other resources devoted to frugality, you really want to have some mentors who live in your community because they'll be aware of local resources, including food co-ops, public transportation, shared housing opportunities, thrift stores, and inexpensive entertainments. You'll often find them in arts, activist, and co-housing communities. Chances are, in fact, that you already know someone who's rocking their frugality, so figure out who that is and ask them for advice.

42. The Only Thing More Precious Than Your Time

The only thing more precious than your time is your **cognitive capacity**, roughly defined as the amount of information you're able to work with at any given moment. We all have only a limited amount, and everything we do, think about, and emotionally deal with uses up some. The goal is to maximize the amount you can devote to your important projects, including, of course, your vocation. (Also, your important personal "projects," such as your health and relationships.)

Happily, whenever you remove a time expense or other low-value activity from your schedule, you reclaim not just the time but the cognitive capacity you would have otherwise devoted to it. Free your time, in other words, and you also free your mind.

You also reclaim cognitive capacity when you overcome procrastination and perfectionism, because both, when present, tend to be ongoing sources of worry. Plus, many perfectionist characteristics, including the tendencies to overcomplicate your projects and work with inadequate resources, will also increase your projects' "cognitive overhead."

Excellent self-care, including good nutrition and abundant sleep and exercise, will also help you maximize your available cognitive capacity, and so can planning and routines. (For instance, going to the gym at the same time each day.) When Flaubert famously said, "Be regular and orderly in your life like a bourgeois so that you may be violent and original in your work," he meant that you should preserve your precious time, energy, and cognitive capacity for your important projects.

Recovering, even partially, from a physical or mental illness can help you reclaim some of your cognitive capacity, and so can coping (again, even partially) with a disability, learning difference, or constraining force such as poverty or bias.

Happily, the more cognitive capacity you reclaim, the more you're often able to reclaim. Every time you solve a problem, for instance, you reclaim the cognitive capacity (and time, money, energy, and other resources) you had been using to cope with it, all of which you can then apply to other problems or projects. This is even better news than it sounds, because **some of our most difficult problems are difficult mainly because we're not setting aside enough time and cognitive capacity to deal with them**. Many who struggle with health and fitness-related goals, for instance, underestimate how much work it takes to change your habits and maintain a healthy lifestyle. The "simple" act of changing your diet, for instance, might require that you read up on nutrition (or consult a nutritionist), figure out a meal plan, research shopping options, and become a more careful shopper and meal preparer. It could also involve seeing a therapist about any emotional eating you're doing, and changing your relationships so that you're mostly hanging out with people who encourage healthy eating.

The first thing to do, therefore, if you have a seemingly intractable problem, is to set aside some time to think, research, and make a plan for solving it. Don't, in other words, make the common mistake of thinking that you should already have a plan before setting the time aside.

Another really excellent way to conserve cognitive capacity is to specialize, a technique I discuss in the next chapter.

Exercise 20

Is there a personal or professional problem that you've been trying to solve but haven't made much progress on? If so, consider whether you've actually invested sufficient time and cognitive capacity in solving it. ("Solving" means things like research, planning, discussions with mentors, and trying out solutions; and not simply spending time worrying or feeling bad about it.) If you haven't invested sufficient resources, do so now.

Sometimes, when people do this exercise, they realize that the "problem" they've been feeling bad about isn't actually a priority. They haven't been procrastinating, in other words—they've been prioritizing. If that's what you've been doing, that's terrific! Keep in mind, however, that perfectionism can cause us to feel bad even about this. (It's grandiosity—the idea that you should be able to handle everything—plus that whole "confusing success and failure" thing.) If that's the case for you, use Chapter 23's loss-acceptance work to neutralize any residual feelings of guilt or disappointment.

43. Specialize!

At work and elsewhere, the most valuable people are often those with a deep specialty who are also able to collaborate effectively with others. Please note that "deep": if you haven't systematically studied your specialty, preferably under the tutelage of someone with excellent real-world experience, and/or worked alongside an exceptional mentor, you're probably not quite there. Strive for those deep learning opportunities.

Productivity-wise, specialization is the bomb. It makes your work easier; saves you loads of time, energy, and cognitive capacity; helps you to develop your expertise; maximizes your enjoyment of your work; and makes you a desirable team member and a natural leader. (Because all that expertise and joy attracts others.) In other words, it's a key to success. Back in my journalism days, I interviewed a CEO who had built his company up from nothing to hundreds of millions of dollars in annual revenue. When I asked him how he did that, he said, "We focused relentlessly on our unique value-add." (His company was an early leader in PC-based computer graphics, and they leveraged that early lead into global dominance.)

In other words: they specialized.

Specialization is particularly important for small business owners because even a tiny business is a more-than-full time endeavor. Trying to "sell all things to all people" is a common newbie error, and a quick road to exhaustion and burnout. (Plus, it confuses your customers and doesn't inspire the kind of trust that helps them feel comfortable handing over their hard-earned dollars to you.) On the other hand, if you become the go-to person in your area for, say, a particular type of tricky upholstery work, or the kind of calculus tutoring that boosts test scores, or the kinds of scrumptious vegan pastries that win taste tests, *that's* the start of a potentially successful business model. (But just the start: you've still got to market and sell effectively and, above all, figure out how to do it all profitably.)

When we specialize, we're usually leveraging our strengths, which is always a good idea. And we're also usually having fun! (Because we tend to enjoy what we're good at, and vice versa.) The Germans have yet another great word for the special kind of pleasure you get from doing something you're good at: *funktionslust*. Specialize, and you'll enjoy lots of it.

Sometimes others are better at spotting our specialties than we are. A wise student changed his entire research focus after a mentor heard him speaking about a different topic and pointed out, "You light up when you [talk about] that."[50] You should also take that kind of feedback seriously—and, obviously, it's also very helpful feedback to give someone else.

If you're having trouble choosing a specialty, you might be self-censoring. We sometimes do that when we're afraid of failing at our specialty, or think others might oppose it. Self-censorship often manifests as ambivalence, so see Chapter 24 for solutions. Or, you might be one of those naturally enthusiastic types with many interests, in which case you'll probably need to make some tough choices and mourn the consequent losses, as discussed in Chapter 23. (Although if you journal about it, the choice might turn out to not be so tough: "I can live, for now, without doing A, B, and C, but I *really* don't want to give up D, so I guess D's my specialty.")

Perhaps you're perfectionistically attached to the idea that you can, or should, be able to "do it all." Science fiction writer Robert Heinlein really went for the perfectionist gold with this passage from his novel *Time Enough for Love*:

> A human being should be able to change a diaper, plan an invasion, butcher a hog, conn a ship, design a building, write a sonnet, balance accounts, build a wall, set a bone, comfort the dying, take orders, give orders, cooperate, act alone, solve equations, analyze a new problem, pitch manure, program a computer, cook a tasty meal, fight efficiently, die gallantly. Specialization is for insects.

Like most perfectionist harangues, it has a certain superficial appeal, but on closer examination makes no sense. Not only does almost no one need to know most of the things on Heinlein's list—plan an invasion? Really!?—we actually do want our bones set by, buildings designed by, and computers programmed by specialists. To add to the general ridiculousness, Heinlein gave that speech to his character Lazarus Long, a mutant human

---

[50] https://uvamagazine.org/articles/first_gens_first

who lives thousands of years, and therefore has literally millennia to learn whatever useful and useless things he wants.

But we don't have those millennia: and so, I much prefer Jane Austen's sensible take in *Pride and Prejudice,* when her protagonist, Lizzie Bennet, after hearing the snobbish Mr. Darcy and Miss Bingley rattle off a voluminous list of things a woman must know to be "truly accomplished"—including "a thorough knowledge of music, singing, drawing, dancing, and the modern languages"—tells Darcy, "I'm no longer surprised at your knowing only six accomplished women. I rather wonder now at your knowing any."

You can also, and should, specialize in your personal life. For a life of vividness, intensity, joy, and true camaraderie, organize your free time around the (replenishing) recreational activities you love most, while at the same time investing in the best equipment, classes, excursions, etc. you can afford. If hiking is your passion, for instance, don't just settle for "okay" local hikes. Do your best to take wonderful hikes in amazing places, with excellent equipment, and in the company of other devoted hikers.

Also, specialize when it comes time to help out friends and relatives. If a friend asks you to help them move, for instance, figure out which part of that process you're best at and help with that. (It could be the packing, the heavy lifting, or the unpacking and organizing of their new home. Or you could be the one who takes care of their dog or cat while it's all going on.) When assisting an ailing or homebound friend or relative, figure out how you can best use your time to support them. Don't trudge to the grocery store or pharmacy, for instance, if you can order online and have everything delivered. And don't mow their lawn or shovel their driveway if you can hire a kid to do it cheap.[51] Instead, offer higher-value support, like escorting your loved one to a medical appointment or helping them with their insurance paperwork. Even a fun afternoon of lunch and Rummikub is a better use of your time and energy than running around doing a lot of chores that someone else could have easily handled.

Finally, also be sure to specialize in your activism / organizing / community work. Figure out what you're good at and focus on that, while also being sure to work alongside other effective people—and only on projects likely to create impact or change. (Usually, those two conditions go hand-in-hand, since effective people tend to seek out impactful projects.)

---

[51] Some nonprofits offer grocery delivery and other services to homebound people: check with the local senior citizens' center and religious organizations, and also the city or county offices for the aged and/or disabled.

44. The Joys of Declining and Delegating

You mostly want to say no to ("decline") any tasks, projects, and other opportunities that aren't your specialty. Even within your specialty, you'll want to decline most of them, keeping only the best—meaning, the most interesting, important, impactful, fun, relevant, and/or strategic—for yourself. That way, your work itself will keep getting more interesting, important, impactful, fun, relevant, and/or strategic.

Unfortunately, many people have trouble saying no, either because they're afraid of disappointing others or grandiosely think that they should be able to "do it all." (Both of which apply to poor Eric in Chapter 1.) If you're one of them, now's the time to break the habit, because saying no isn't just a productivity skill, it's a profound form of self-care *and* one of life's great pleasures. (One of my favorite memes is the one with the woman snug in bed with her cat, both of them propped up on many pillows in television-watching position. Meanwhile, she's saying to someone on the phone, "Yeah, can't come out tonight. Super busy.")[52]

A reluctance to say no can also lead to overgiving, a seriously self-sabotaging behavior I discuss in the next chapter.

So practice saying no. Do it with small and easy requests at first, and then larger and tougher ones, until you're entirely comfortable saying it even to people who pressure you. Also, **work on getting past needing a "good reason" to say no** (like a deadline or test). You want to get comfortable saying no for the simple reason that, "it's not a good fit for me."

---

[52] https://ifunny.co/picture/sorry-can-t-come-out-tonight-super-busy-XhrUnKBr8. See also: https://anildash.com/2012/07/19/jomo/.

44. The Joys of Declining and Delegating

Delegation, or getting someone else to do part of a task, is the other great time-reclamation skill. It's often thought of narrowly as something supervisors do "to" their subordinates, but you can do it more equitably by: (a) delegating tasks to those for whom they are a specialty, and (b) providing lots of support and mentoring while they're working. When you delegate this way, you're actually creating many great outcomes along with just reclaiming your time, including strengthening your relationship with the person helping you, and helping them develop their own skills.

You can also pay someone to help you. I'm actually a big fan of this if you can afford it. As discussed in Chapter 39, time is more valuable than money, and so it makes sense to use your money to "buy time." (It's also good to help a good person earn their living.) Also, since the person you're paying is hopefully an expert, paying is often the quickest and easiest way to get really great support. Paying someone to tutor you on a difficult subject for an hour or two each week, versus struggling for many more hours on your own, is a great investment, especially given that you're likely to learn more from the tutoring than your solitary struggles. Ditto for paying someone to fix your computer, versus spending days or weeks trying to fix it yourself. (Or worse, trying to live with the flakiness.)

Again, this is all contingent on your having enough cash. I know many people don't, but I also know, from my classes and elsewhere, that many people who actually do have the ability to pay for help are reluctant to do that. Please do not make that mistake.

Issues of payment aside, people often have lots of reasons why they "can't" delegate a particular task—or *any* task—including:

- "It's such a little thing that I might as well do it myself." (Nope! Your time is precious.)
- "I can do it better myself." (Even if that's true—and often it's not—it's usually better, from an overall efficiency standpoint, to delegate.)
- "I don't have anyone to delegate to." (Help is abundant. You may have to search a bit to find the right person, but believe me: that person is out there.)

Regardless of how compelling the justification sounds, you'll often find, at the root of a reluctance to delegate, a plain old reluctance to ask for help, as discussed in Chapter 10.

Another reason to embrace both declining and delegating is that, as noted in Chapter 38, success makes you busier. Each of your professional and personal accomplishments is likely to result in yet more invitations, ideas, projects, potential partnerships, and other opportunities arriving at your door. Don't get me wrong: this is a great problem to have! But it's still a problem. Say "yes" to even just a few too many and you'll quickly run aground. So yeah: you want to get entirely comfortable declining and delegating all but the very best that's offered to you.

Please remember that a good delegator must also be a good manager. Bad managers throw a task at someone and don't want to hear from them again until it's completed. Good managers, in contrast, take as much time as needed to explain things fully at the beginning of the project; then check in with their helper regularly while the work is underway. And after the project is done, they offer feedback. The math might initially look something like this: you invest three hours supervising someone you're delegating to, and they then spend five, or eight, or ten hours doing the actual work—so you've "gained" between two and seven hours of their time. (Obviously, if it's a repetitive task, the amount of time reclaimed is even higher.) Even if your gain is just an hour or two, however, it's still worth delegating. Remember that delegating offers many yields besides just the time reclaimed, and that Good Time Managers value small time increments.

Good delegators are also kind and patient and otherwise nonperfectionist.

So work to become a frequent decliner and delegator. Of course, if you do, then sooner or later you'll either decline a task you should have taken on, or delegate a task to the wrong person. These inevitable mistakes are *not* a reason to stop declining and delegating, but rather to work on improving your process. (And also your ability to tolerate "failure," see Chapter 22.)

45. The Perils of Overgiving

Overgiving is when you frequently take on tasks, projects, relationships, and other commitments that you should decline. At the very least, it's a pernicious form of Quasiproductive Procrastination. But often it's even worse than that. Here's what can happen when you overgive at your job, or to a group you belong to, or to a person:
- You're so busy doing their stuff that you don't have time to do your own.
- You're stressed, exhausted, and resentful.
- You're possibly also broke—because many overgivers are also too free with their money.
- Dangerously, you attract the wrong people: those looking, consciously or unconsciously, for someone to exploit.

While many overgivers are motivated by a sincere desire to help, the problem is also often rooted in perfectionism ("I should be able to do it all!") and an unwillingness to say no. Some may also get an ego boost from being a "problem solver," "go-to person," or even—although they'd never say this word aloud—"savior." (Grandiose much?) Many fall into the trap of **workaholism**, which psychologists characterize as an addictive/escapist behavior linked to stress, depression, ill health, and impaired personal relationships. Workaholics may work long hours but their accomplishments often fall short, both because their underlying motivation is escape (versus effectiveness or efficiency), and because their lack of life balance is sabotaging.

Sadly, many organizations encourage and exploit people's tendency to overgive. Many health, educational, and community organizations are seriously understaffed, thus forcing their employees to constantly have to choose between maintaining their own healthy boundaries and meeting the legitimate, and often serious, needs of their patients, students, or clients. Many social justice organizations are likewise happy to exploit activists' guilt over taking any time off from fixing society's urgent problems. (It's especially shameful when organizations with a social justice mission exploit workers or volunteers.)

The solutions to overgiving are to work on your perfectionism, make sure you're doing things for the right motives, learn to say no and delegate, and consult a therapist if the problem persists. Also, find great mentors and learn from them. Many experienced health care workers, teachers, and others have learned how to work effectively while also maintaining healthy boundaries; and many experienced activists, as noted in Chapter 40, see self-care and life balance as foundational. Finally, time budgeting (Chapter 46) and scheduling (Chapter 47) are crucial because, in their absence, overgiving—like escapism and chores—often expands to fill any and all available time.

Operating Principles are also useful for overcoming overgiving, as well as for generally managing your time, relationships, and other priorities. An operating principle is a short, easily-remembered mantra or "rule to live by" that you use to make better decisions, especially under pressure. Some work-related examples:

- "X and Y are my responsibilities; Z isn't. Whenever someone asks me to do Z, I *always* direct them to the person in charge of that."
- "On weeknights I'm in bed by midnight—no exceptions."
- "I always shut off my phone while working."

And three more general ones:

- "Perfectionism is always a dead end, so I never go there."
- "With very limited exceptions, I only volunteer to help people when I can do so using my specialties."
- "When I'm in conflict with someone, I always respond with kindness."

The intensifiers—"always," "no exceptions," "never," "very," and "only"—are there to remind you to adhere to the operating principle even when you're tempted not to. It's not that you can never override an operating principle: you just need a really good reason for doing so. (You can also always revise or eliminate an operating principle if it's not working for you.)

You come up with your operating principles by researching your field's best practices, and also by observing your mentors and having discussions with them. You can also figure them out as you go along. Many Good Time Managers (GTMs), for instance, after having gotten mired in a bad collaboration, adopt the operating principle, "If someone I'm working with is unreliable or otherwise difficult, I end my work with them as soon as possible and *never* work with them again." And many performers, after having been burned by promises of "payment" in exposure or publicity that didn't pan out, adopt an operating principle similar to, "I *never* work for free, no matter how worthy or prominent the event is." (They might make an exception for one charity or cause they especially care about.)

Overcoming Email/Messaging/Collaborative Apps Overload

Email, messaging, and collaborative apps are tricky, from a productivity standpoint, for several reasons:
- They combine the spontaneity of verbal communication with the permanence of written communication.
- The lack of nonverbal content, like vocal tone and body language, can cause confusion and misinterpretation.
- We email and message all kinds of people for all kinds of reasons, so it's hard to come up with a set of general rules.
- We get so many emails and messages that if we overwork each one even just a tiny bit, it can still add up to a lot of misused time.

Email/collaborative apps overload can also be at least partly an overgiving problem, because many people spend too much time on their emails for fear of looking bad or disappointing others.

The solutions are the same as for general overgiving—reduce your perfectionism, understand your motives, and develop some operating principles. In addition:
- **Reply tersely.** Not every decision requires an explanation, and it's often when we're explaining, or trying to, that things get out of hand. Explanations can quickly turn into essays, and feeling like you have to write an essay—especially when you didn't mean to, don't need to, and don't want to—can lead to frustration and procrastination. And

even when we do manage to get the essay out, that will likely encourage the other person to respond with an equally long explanation of their own, which adds still more unnecessary work.

Instead of writing long explanations, therefore, try sending messages like this: "OK, thanks," and "Yes, thanks—please let me know if you have questions." Also, as per the last chapter, "It's not a good fit for me, but thanks for asking." (In cases where you feel an explanation is truly necessary, it's often quicker to communicate verbally.)

- **Abstain from replying.** Not every message requires a response.
- **Learn from mentors.** Many successful professionals have techniques for keeping their emails and messaging under control. They might, for instance, set a strict time limit on their daily email/collaborative software use, which encourages them to be efficient. Or they might affix a signature line to all their outgoing messages letting correspondents know that not all messages will be answered. Speaking of which...
- **Use your tech.** Autoresponders can be set up to automatically reply to routine queries. (This also helps ensure an accurate and consistent response.) Filters can be set up to separate out urgent from nonurgent emails—and maybe you only check the "nonurgent" folder once or twice a week. Customizing your email and messaging apps to boost your efficiency is an excellent time investment that can yield an incredible return over the years.

Overuse of **social media** is also often at least partly an overgiving problem. If you're sticking with a boring, stressful, or otherwise unproductive conversation (or platform) because others will be hurt or angry if you leave, that's overgiving. Ask yourself, therefore, whether you're giving too much of your precious time, energy, and cognitive capacity to online people, conversations, topics, groups, and apps that aren't giving you much back. If the answer's yes, then leave as soon as you can.

About Boundaries

There are four things you need to know about interpersonal boundaries from a time-management perspective:
1. The important "boundary" isn't between you and the other person but within you. It's how you define your relationship with that person, and especially your obligations and responsibilities to them.

45. The Perils of Overgiving

2. **You should make conscious choices about your boundaries.** Do this even in relationships with a lot of personal and societal expectations, such as those with family members. Don't, in other words, automatically buy into clichés or traditions about how you're supposed to behave.
3. **It's your responsibility to state your needs.** Often, others don't even know that there's a problem until we tell them—and when we do, they often surprise us with their supportiveness. ("Oh, so you need to skip some of the holiday events so you can finish your project? No problem!") Sooner or later, however, you'll probably encounter someone who isn't so supportive, which brings us to...
4. **Distance yourself from unsupportive people.** And give serious thought as to whether you even want them in your life.

These kinds of decisions, and the ensuing conversations, can be among the most difficult and unpleasant aspects of time management. But defending your boundaries isn't just an essential life skill, it's a profound form of self-care. If you find yourself struggling with this, it might also help to remember that, **in a world filled with Poor Time Managers (PTMs)—not to mention, the occasional clueless or callous person—disappointing people is a sign that you're doing your time management right.**

Also remember that GTMs are problem-solvers and optimizers who don't settle for partial solutions. They also tend to be clear on the long-term consequences of their actions—or, perhaps more to the point, *in*actions. So, while a PTM might be reluctant to disappoint someone by declining an offer, "impose" on them by delegating, or "upset" them by defending their boundaries, a GTM clearly sees the consequences of being reticent, and this motivates them to act.

Kids Rock!

As mentioned in Chapter 35, we often don't have enough faith in the people around us; and once we actually do ask our family, friends, supervisors, colleagues, etc., for support, they provide it—and often more of it than we had asked for.

You know who really rocks the whole support thing—not to mention, the timed work intervals (Chapter 6), obstacle resolution process (Chapter 9), and other techniques in this book? Kids. Here are a couple of fun examples from my classes:

- Dad, a would-be entrepreneur, had a conundrum: after a full day of work and school, he had to write his business plan at night. But his four-year-old daughter, having not seen him all day, wanted—no, demanded—his full attention. (And, of course, he wanted to spend time with her as well.) Now, Dad was a former Marine and a tough-looking guy: you got the impression that he had no trouble setting boundaries in other areas of his life. But, entertainingly to me and the rest of the class, he seemed in thrall to his tiny daughter. Encouraged to include her in his problem-solving, he finally confessed his dilemma to her, saying something like (as he reported to us in class the next day), "Daddy loves spending time with you but he also has to do his homework. What should we do?" Daughter thought the question over carefully before deciding, "We can do our homework together." It was a great solution! From then on, they worked side-by-side at the dining room table, he on his business planning, and she on her drawing and other projects. (He also reported that she checked up on him periodically, just to make sure he was making good progress.)
- Mom, a graduate student who also worked a part-time job, had a similar problem: she had a lot of homework, most of which she needed to do at night after her six-year-old son went to bed, but he wanted "endless" bedtime stories. Encouraged to be candid with him about her dilemma, she told him that, while she loved their shared time together, she was sad because she wasn't getting her work done. Like Daughter, above, Son came up with a great solution: that they limit themselves to one bedtime story on weeknights. Then–plot twist! The first night they did this, Mom felt bad about limiting Son to one story, and suggested they read another. Son, she reported the next day, looked her right in the eye and said, "Shouldn't you be doing your homework?" It turned out that, while Mom truly did enjoy reading bedtime stories to Son, she was also using the task to procrastinate on her own work.

Involve your kids in your time-budgeting and other problem-solving, and you'll soon realize that parenting doesn't have to be, and shouldn't be, zero sum, with all your needs and goals being sacrificed to those of your children. In fact, **one of the greatest gifts you can give your kids is to let them watch you wrestle with these kinds of difficult time management decisions, modeling for them how to live a life of love and responsibility and commitment without sacrificing one's dreams.**

45. The Perils of Overgiving

Meanwhile, as our kids get older, they often require less of our time—so don't just assume, for instance, that your teen wants you to attend all their sports games: ask them.

Again, I recommend Faber and Mazlish's *How to Talk so Kids Will Listen & Listen So Kids Will Talk* as a guide to having the above kinds of conversations.

Exercise 21

You've already sent out some fun Intentionally Erroneous Emails (Exercise 10) to help with your perfectionism. Now it's time to send out some Intentionally Terse Emails to help with your overgiving, as per the discussion in this chapter. So go ahead and do that!

Exercise 22

Start creating your lists of professional and personal operating principles. Write down a few you're already living by, and post the list prominently so you can review and edit it frequently. Especially when something doesn't go as planned, think of what you might have done differently and see if you can turn that insight into an operating principle.

Okay, we're done discussing the ideas underlying time management. On to the process itself...

46. Budgeting Your Time

As already noted, you need to budget, schedule, and (at least for a while) track your time. We discuss budgeting in this chapter, and scheduling and tracking in the next.

Budgeting is the act of defining your priorities and determining how much time, each week, you'll devote to each. Sounds simple, but, as you will see, it can involve some tough choices and deep thought. Here's how you do it:

1. Start by acknowledging that sleep deprivation isn't a valid time-management strategy.[53] Then, admit to how much sleep you truly need each night and commit to getting that sleep. (For most of us, that will be around seven or eight hours.) Then, subtract your week's total sleep from 168, the total number of hours in a week. If you need seven hours of sleep a night, for instance, that's 49 hours of sleep a week, leaving 119 hours a week of "awake" time. That may sound like a lot, but just wait...

2. Create your ideal weekly time budget. That's the budget you would use if you had unlimited time each week. We start with your ideal budget so that you can look at your time use with fresh eyes and come up with a budget that reflects your true priorities. (Many time management systems begin by having you examine your current patterns of time use but I think doing so risks skewing the result. So, let's skip that step.) This is the step in the time-management process where you

---

[53] If this article doesn't convince you to get enough sleep, I don't know what will: http://www.theguardian.com/lifeandstyle/2019/feb/09/best-thing-you-can-do-for-your-health-sleep-well. I especially like the author's call to, "Reclaim our right to a full night of sleep, without embarrassment or the terrible stigma of laziness."

go wild! If you dream of working a full-time job and participating in several community groups, while at the same time building your business, hitting the gym every day, maintaining a fabulous home, and being present at every one of your kids' school events, list it all and record the number of hours it will all take.

Some tips:
- It's easiest to do this on a spreadsheet template, and I provide one at https://www.hillaryrettigproductivity.com/.
- Remember that, in Values-Based Time Management, we manage our personal as well as our professional time. You should therefore be sure to include your personal activities and projects in your budget and, later, in your scheduling and tracking.
- Be sure to budget at least some time for all the Investment Categories listed in Chapter 40.
- Be sure to include travel and prep time for each activity. For example, when budgeting for your workout, include the time it takes to travel to and from the gym, change into your workout clothes (and then back into your ordinary clothes afterwards), and shower.
- For biweekly, monthly, and other non-weekly commitments, just budget the average weekly time. (A four-hour monthly appointment would be budgeted for an hour a week.) Your schedule won't work out exactly, but doing this works well enough—especially if you underschedule, see below—and it is much easier than trying to work out a "perfect" budget that accounts for every minute.

When you're done, add up the hours per week. If you're like most people, your ideal time budget will come in at around 150 to 200 hours per week. Time to cut...

3. Eliminate as many of your time expenses from your budget as you can. I offered some suggestions for this in Chapter 41, including quitting unwanted activities and relationships, delegating or outsourcing chores, cutting back on escapism, and being frugal. But maybe you can come up with some others. Be ruthless! The goal—which no one ever actually achieves but is still worth aiming for—is zero time expenses, with all your time going to investments.

If you can't eliminate an expense entirely, trim it down. (Recall that Good Time Managers, GTMs, are optimizers who value small increments of their precious time; also, that the small cuts add up over time.) If you can cut fifteen minutes from an expense, you absolutely should do that.

When you're done eliminating and trimming expenses, add up all your commitments again. Hopefully, you're now much closer to 119 hours.

4. Sort your investments into three groups: high-, medium-, and low-priority. High-priority investments are those you must do and those you really want to do. Low-priority ones are those you could live without. The medium-priority ones will be somewhere in the middle. Yes, your rankings will probably be somewhat arbitrary and imprecise, but in the process of doing this, you'll give serious thought to, and make tough decisions about, what's truly important to you. A major aim of time management is to make these kinds of difficult, yet vital, decisions consciously and deliberately in advance, instead of impulsively during a scheduling conflict, the way Poor Time Managers (PTMs) do.

I think you know what's coming next...

5. Eliminate as many of the low-priority investments from your time budget as you can. And any that you can't eliminate, trim as much as you can. Just be careful not to eliminate any of the investment *categories* entirely from your budget, however. It's important to do at least some self-care, relationship care, education, vocational work, replenishing recreation, activism, and planning and management every week. (As noted in Chapter 40, some activities (e.g., socializing) belong to more than one category, and some categories may be subsumed into others, such as when you do some education as part of your vocation or planning.)

When you're done eliminating and trimming your low-value investments, add up all your commitments again. Probably, you're now even closer to 119 hours, but still not there. So now it's time to...

6. Eliminate, or trim, your medium-priority investments. This is the point at which budgeting can get challenging, because now you're cutting back on some stuff you really want to be doing. You could, for instance, be asking yourself to give up an exciting community project, or a couple of fun workouts a week, or a night or two of socializing that you really value. It may help to remind yourself that productivity work is all about getting real, and pretending that you have the time to do something when you really don't is not an option.

Postponing, however, is sometimes an option. I once knew someone who was trying to write her thesis at the same time she was working full-time *and* training for a marathon. Needless to say, she wasn't making much progress. "Thesis now, marathon later," I suggested. Presto! Progress on thesis!

You're probably even closer to your 119 hours now. But you're probably not quite there (because there are so many investments that need to be squeezed into the week). So now it's time to...

7. Trim your high-priority investments. Budgeting now becomes an almost Buddhist discipline, forcing you to acknowledge and accept what may be life's most painful reality, our tragically limited amount of time. It will probably help if you take some time to mourn your losses, as discussed in Chapter 23; also, if you remember that you're making these sacrifices for the best possible reason: your personal liberation. **Please also remember that, when all is said and done, you'll probably have enough time to do everything you need to do, and even much of what you want to do, if you use your time well.** GTMs derive some solace and motivation from that truth but it's often lost on the poor PTMs, who remain in stubborn denial about both their time constraints and the potential of time management to mitigate their losses. So, they struggle on under the delusion that if they could only somehow, magically, "get their act together," they'd be able to "do it all."

GTMs also know that the goal isn't to squeeze every possible activity into our time budget but, rather. to eliminate as many of the less-essential and inessential activities as possible, so that we have abundant time—or, as abundant as possible—for the essentials. Or, put another way: **an important time management strategy is to not have too many activities to manage in the first place.**

8. When you arrive at your goal (e.g., 119 hours), take a moment to stop and appreciate the achievement. It's a meaningful one.

But you're not quite done yet...

The Genius of Underscheduling

I always advise people to try for a "98% budget"—meaning, to leave two or three hours open and unscheduled each week. Underscheduling helps you accommodate both the unexpected tasks, like when someone needs your help, and also the irregular (biweekly, monthly, etc.) ones.

PTMs, sadly, resist doing it. Chronically behind in their work and other obligations, perfectionistically attached to suffering and pressure, and grandiosely refusing to accept their time limitations—not to mention, the laws of physics (you can't be in two places at once)—they have a strong compulsion to schedule every single moment of their lives.

With all that in mind, let's return to our budgeting process:

9. Cut and trim some more. A good goal to aim for would be anywhere from three to five unscheduled hours per week.
Finally, we have an important step that many people forget...
10. Show your time budget to your mentor(s). And ask the all-important question, "Am I using my time in the right way to achieve my goals?" This will not only get you some valuable feedback, it will show your mentor that you're really on the ball.

Sample Weekly Time Budget

Table III, below, shows a sample time budget for a parent with the usual family obligations, who also has a part-time job and is working on a vocation (writing, art, school, entrepreneurship, community organizing, etc.). This example presumes that there is a partner or spouse who is the primary breadwinner, so this parent isn't under pressure to earn a high salary; also, that the children are older and at school all day.[54]

---

[54] Obviously, not everyone has the luxury of two household incomes. Although some single parents do manage to pursue their vocation while also working at a job and raising their children, that's a pretty heavy load, time-wise. If you're trying to do this, that's great, but if it ever starts to feel overwhelming, rework your time budget until it's more manageable. That will probably involve some hard choices, but remember that productivity work is all about getting real—and that nothing will sabotage your goals faster than exhaustion and burnout. Also, don't forget, as discussed in Chapter 45, to involve your kids and other stakeholders in your time-management process.

Table III: Sample Weekly Time Budget for a Working Parent With Vocation

Activity	Hrs/Week*	Notes
Job	24	Hopefully, a low-stress job with an easy commute. Bonus points if it supports their vocational goals. (E.g., an artist might work at acommunity arts center, gallery, frame shop, or arts supply store.)
Self-Care	14.5	An hour per day for grooming and other personal care, plus 7.5 hours a week for exercise (e.g., three yoga classes).
Vocation	25	Art, entrepreneurship, etc. (Includes some education, e.g., taking a class related to your endeavor.)
Meals	14	A half-hour for all breakfasts and lunches, and an hour for all dinners (includes cooking and cleanup time).
Socializing/ Recreation	20	Family activities (hopefully replenishing), plus a date night with partner / spouse.
Escapism	10.5	1.5 hours per day for social media, gaming, television, etc., some of it presumably with family. (See Chapter 41.)
Chores and Errands	4	Laundry, shopping, cleaning, etc. This person knows they must be efficient, and are delegating / outsourcing whenever possible. (Hopefully others in the household are also doing their share.)
Community Work	2	Whichever cause you care most about. If community work is the vocation, then this time can be reallocated.
Planning / Management	2	Includes research and meetings with mentors, etc. Also, reviewing the week's time use, as per Chapter 47.
Total	116	(Out of 119 hours total = underscheduling!)

*All time estimates include commuting and preparation time.

This schedule is an example only: yours is likely to be different even if your family and personal circumstances are similar to those described. Note that all the investment categories are covered.

Exercise 23

Go ahead and create your own Time Budget using the process outlined in this chapter. Take your time and pay attention to your feelings, especially while cutting and trimming activities. If you feel sad or conflicted about not being able to do everything you'd like, that probably means you're doing your budgeting right. Use the solutions discussed above and in Chapter 23 to help process those feelings.

47. Scheduling and Tracking Your Time

After finishing your Time Budget, your next step is to create a weekly schedule. Download a form for this from https://www.hillaryrettigproductivity.com or photocopy a page from a daily planner. Then use this process:
1. Fill in your obligatory commitments: job, family obligations, etc.
2. Figure out when, during the day, you're at your highest energy, and schedule your priorities (e.g., your vocation) then. Also, your exercise and any other priorities that you find challenging or might be tempted to skip. Keep this time sacred for those activities, doing your best to never, ever schedule anything else during it.
3. As much as possible, schedule your vocational work and other important tasks in chunks of an hour or more. You need these chunks because: (a) interruptions are "expensive" time-wise (as discussed in Chapter 5), (b) it can take a while to immerse ourselves in a task—although nonperfectionism can help to reduce that immersion time a lot, and (c) because tough creative and intellectual challenges usually require sustained focus and concentration.
4. Set up routines—meaning that, whenever possible, you should try to do the same thing at the same time and in the same place each day. This sounds boring but, as discussed in Chapter 42, it simplifies your life and helps you conserve your precious time, energy, and cognitive capacity.
5. Bonus points, as always, for showing your work to your mentors and asking for feedback.

Tracking

Once you've developed your schedule, you should start using it. And, for a while, at least, you should track your time use. Tracking helps you to be mindful of your time use, thus making it easier for you to stick to your schedule. Here's how to do it:

1. Download the tracking form from https://www.hillaryrettigproductivity.com Or create your own from a spreadsheet. It should be a grid with columns for Monday through Sunday and a row for each of your activities, including your personal ones. Also, a row to record any procrastination you do each day—Don't worry! No judgments here.—and other rows to record the time you wake up and go to bed each day. Finally, there should be a Total box at the end of every column and row, and a box for recording Notes at the end of each row, after the Total.
2. Keep the sheet with you, in either electronic or printed form, as you go through your day.
3. *Every fifteen minutes*, put a check mark on the activity you just worked on. So, if you do two hours of music practice on Monday, you'll have entered eight check marks in the "Monday/Music" box. You track every fifteen minutes for two important reasons: (a) it's easy to forget what you've done, even an hour later, and (b) frequent check-ins keep you alert and mindful of your time use, thus helping you to stay on schedule.
4. Record any time you spend procrastinating. Record how long you procrastinated, what activity you used to procrastinate, and why you think you did it. (The last two should go in the Notes box—and feel free to expand on this analysis using Chapter 9's Obstacle Identification and Resolution technique.)
5. Also record your daily wake-up and go-to-bed times. It's best, from the standpoint of both your productivity and your health, to wake up and go to bed at about the same time every day. (Otherwise, you're basically giving yourself jet lag.)
6. Midway through your week, check for rows with few or no check marks—meaning, tasks you've skimped on, or maybe skipped entirely. Be sure to devote some time to those.
7. At the end of the week, add up all the horizontal and vertical totals and record those in the appropriate boxes. Then, analyze the results and, if needed, make a plan to do better next week. Do this by first noting and appreciating the times you followed your schedule and got

your work done. Then, nonperfectionistically (without judgments or punishments) look at all the times you derailed, and see if you can figure out why—and how to avoid those derailments in the future. (Again, use the Obstacle Identification and Resolution technique.) If needed, tweak your budget and schedule so that they better fit the realities of your time use: they're "living" documents that you should feel free to change at any time as your needs, situation, and priorities change.

8. Repeat the entire process the following week.

Some people track for just a couple of weeks after starting with a new schedule, just to get used to it and to identify any changes that need to be made. Others track for their whole career—or beyond, if they're also tracking their personal time. And some track just in a few key areas. (I continue to track my writing and exercise times, just to make sure that, no matter what else is happening in my life, those crucial tasks get done.) Do whatever works for you.

As you optimize your time use, you should hopefully find yourself feeling not just more productive, but happier, healthier, and less stressed. Perhaps you'll also notice improvements in your relationships and other important areas of your life. These are all yields that Values-Based Time Management can create; and it's important that you notice them, especially during the early stages of the process, because doing so will help you stay motivated.

Exercise 24

Create a weekly schedule from Exercise 23's Time Budget; then track your time for at least a couple of weeks. Pay particular attention to your emotions and stress level during that time. Hopefully, as you continue to optimize your time use, you'll see yourself getting happier and less stressed.

48. Putting It All Together

Here's what it might look like when you're really rocking your Values-Based Time Management:

Remember Eric from Chapter 1? Well, I'm happy to report that, just a couple of years after his failed attempt to get his Master's degree, he decided to try again. This time, it was a given that he would only take one class at a time—and, for a while, he thought that that would be the only adjustment he needed to make to his plan. Fortunately, he consulted a mentor, Ryan, who was a leading member of one of his networking groups. Ryan was one of those people who always seemed to get lots of high-quality work done while at the same time maintaining a good work-life balance.

Ryan called sticking to one class "a good start" but urged Eric to take his time management efforts to the limit. "You don't want to squeak by with just enough time for your priorities," he said. "The goal is abundant time for them—or, at least, as abundant as possible—so you can do them well without burning out. Go home and create a weekly time budget that does that; then email it to me so we can discuss it."

Eric did so. He thought his first budget was pretty good but Ryan encouraged him to cut more time expenses and lower-priority investments.

He did another revision and sent it. "I think you can cut some more," Ryan insisted.

And so he did a third round.

This time Ryan approved Eric's budget.

Now it was time to make the changes. The first person Eric approached was his supervisor, Tasha. He wasn't surprised when she responded to his plan to return to school with only lukewarm enthusiasm: after all, the last

48. Putting It All Together

time he had combined work and school, he had screwed up an important project. And so, he quickly added, "This time I'm only taking one class."

"Great idea," Tasha said, with a bit more enthusiasm. "How can I help?"

Eric took a deep breath and asked to work four ten-hour days a week, instead of the usual five day/eight-hour schedule; and also to telecommute one of those days. That would not only give him a three-day weekend in which to do his schoolwork but allow him to reclaim several hours each week that would otherwise go to commuting.

Tasha readily agreed to the four-day schedule but was concerned that if Eric telecommuted his work and team performance would suffer. Ryan had told Eric to be prepared to defend his request, and so he resisted the urge to promise to come into the office whenever needed. Instead, he promised to be available via teleconference whenever needed, and also assured Tasha that if the telecommuting didn't work out he'd readily go back to working all four days at the office.

Tasha agreed.

Eric's next challenge was to gracefully exit from a community group he belonged to that met every couple of weeks but wasn't accomplishing much. Truth be told, he had long ago lost interest in it but had been reluctant to leave—partly because he hated to be a "quitter," but mostly because he knew some of the group's members would react badly to his leaving. (He'd seen it happen before.) Ryan suggested that he avoid unhelpful labels like "quitter" and also take the long view. (Was he going to stay in the group forever? If not, might as well get out now.) So, Eric gathered his courage and quit the group. Some people did indeed take his leaving personally, but it turned out not to be such a big deal. And wow, what a relief it was to be free of that ungratifying commitment.

Eric's next step was also hard: he had to explicitly tell certain family members and friends that he would not be as available for socializing while taking a class. He invested time in coming up with messaging that was both kind and clear; and, during the ensuing discussions, resisted the impulse to add qualifying statements like, "But we can get together over the weekend," when he didn't really want to do that. ("Sometimes," Ryan had told him, "You just have to say no.")

Not every time management task was so challenging, though. Eric originally thought he'd have to cut back on his daily gym days, which bummed him out. Ryan, however, advocated for keeping those because it was good for health and stress reduction. He instead suggested a (to Eric) rather shocking alternative: outsourcing and otherwise delegating as many of his household chores and errands as possible. When he made the suggestion, Eric felt a resurgence of his old tendency to want to "do it all." But he now recognized that thinking as perfectionist, and so was willing to give the advice a try.

He started with grocery shopping, a tedious and time-consuming chore. He switched to a supermarket that let him order his groceries online and that also offered free delivery. (Except for the tip, which he was happy to pay.) It was a great convenience and time-saver, and Eric couldn't help wondering why he hadn't made the switch years ago.

Hiring a cleaning person to come in biweekly was a bit more guilt-inducing, at first—and it didn't help that some of his friends ribbed him about it. But it quickly turned out to be a great investment that improved his sense of comfort while at the same time giving him yet more time to devote to his priorities.

Eric reported all these changes back to Ryan, who said he had done a great job at following through.

Eric drew up a schedule and tracked his time for a few weeks, and while he did have to make a few adjustments to his budget and schedule—mostly because he'd been a bit too optimistic about his commuting and prep times—overall things worked out well. He enjoyed his class and did well on all his assignments and tests. He attended all the optional tutorials, and his professor, with whom he met regularly, was very praising of his work.

Of course, Eric had also done his antiperfectionism work—including Timed Work Intervals, Reframing, Dialoguing with His Inner Perfectionist, Abundant Resourcing, Joyful Dance, etc.—so his work pace and output were both excellent.

Meanwhile, Tasha was also happy, both with Eric's availability and his work performance. A few weeks into the semester, she told him she'd have no objection to continuing their four-day workweek/telecommuting arrangement next semester.

Eric was also much happier and healthier, and less stressed, than he had been in years. The knowledge that he was using his time well, and making progress at important goals, led to a real self-esteem boost.

When doing his time management, Eric had had to leave his comfort zone many times: to talk to Ryan, talk to Tasha, leave the community group, get explicit with friends and family about his time constraints, and embrace getting help at home. But the rewards were more than worth it. He felt that he had "leveled up," and it was all due to Values-Based Time Management!

48. Putting It All Together

Like all the work in this book, you want to take your Values-Based Time Management to the max. The harder you rock it, the more benefit you'll receive from it.

Don't settle for being a Good Time Manager, in other words, when you can be a Great Time Manager!

Conclusion
Liberating Yourself and the World

Conclusion: Liberating Yourself and the World

A funny thing happens to many people as they move through life: they start to settle.

They settle for jobs they don't want but that provide a paycheck.

For relationships that bore or stress them but that they can't bring themselves to end.

For towns they don't like, because moving's a hassle.

And for governments and other systems that neglect and exploit them, because "It's always been that way" or, "What can one person do?"

You can watch it happen and, unfortunately, probably will. Decade after decade, you'll see more and more of your contemporaries "settle down" and, in some cases, get stuck.

Please don't let that happen to you.

Now, don't get me wrong: there's no such thing as a perfect outcome, and so everyone does eventually have to settle to some extent. Moreover, difficult times—and I think it's safe to say that we currently are living through some—tend to require even more settling than usual. So don't feel bad about any decisions you need to make, even if they're not the ones you'd make if, say, jobs were more plentiful and better paying, or the political situation more secure.

At the same time, however, don't settle preemptively, or more than you have to. Out there, somewhere, are a career, place, lifestyle, and relationships that will make you happy—or, at least, happier than the alternatives. These are definitely worth working toward and, if necessary, fighting for. And I speak from experience when I say that, even if you're in your 30s, 40s, or beyond, it's not too late to start!

Your life has value and meaning, and not just to you but the rest of us. You may be just one small thread in the vast tapestry that we call life, but you matter. If most of the threads in our tapestry shine, then it will be a vibrant work of beauty. If most don't, then the tapestry, and life itself, will be dull. Best of all, you now have most of what you need to get out there and shine. Nonperfectionism, the Joyful Dance, Values-Based Time Management, and the other techniques in this book will take you far, especially if you use them not just for your work but your play, relationships, and other important areas of your life. And let's add **authenticity** to your list of foundational values. By that I mean that the trajectory of your life, and of your individual days, should align as much as possible with your true goals, values, needs, and desires. Put another way: **you should mostly be doing the things you want to be doing, in the company of those with whom you'd mostly like to be doing them.** (As discussed in Chapter 43, if you focus on the things you love, the community often naturally follows.)

Authenticity isn't a goal so much as a path. You walk it by listening to, and then acting on, that quiet inner voice that tells you what's working and not working for you. Also, you want to cherish and nurture your vision of the ideal career and life you'd like to have. Sure—you don't want to perfectionistically cling to that vision too tightly, or get upset when you fall short of achieving aspects of it. But it should always be there in the background of your thoughts, informing, guiding, and inspiring you. Writer Neil Gaiman offered a terrific example of this in a commencement speech he gave at the University of the Arts:

> Something that worked for me was imagining that where I wanted to be—an author, primarily of fiction, making good books, making good comics and supporting myself through my words—was a mountain. A distant mountain. My goal.
>
> And I knew that as long as I kept walking towards the mountain I would be all right. And when I truly was not sure what to do, I could stop, and think about whether it was taking me towards or away from the mountain. I said no to editorial jobs on magazines, proper jobs that would have paid proper money, because I knew that, attractive though they were, for me they would have been walking away from the mountain.[55]

Do your best to stay on the path, even during—especially during—difficult times. Take bold steps toward your destination when you can, and small steps when you can't. Enjoy the successes and persevere through the

---

[55] https://www.youtube.com/watch?v=2OwRUyZMKwI

setbacks. (And don't dichotomize them: they're all just "station stops" along your life's path.)

Remember that it's your community, more than any other single factor under your direct control, that will determine your success. Surround yourself with supporters, mentors, and encouragers, and they'll likely accelerate your progress. But surround yourself with naysayers, cynics, and *dis*couragers, and you'll likely stall. Even beyond that, you want to live, work, and play, as much as possible, among empowered and effective people, including Good Time Managers, since that will help you build your own empowerment and effectiveness. The goal, really, is to **"live among the wise,"** as the Buddha put it—and it's even more important to do that online than off, so that you can avoid, as much as possible, social media's rampant perfectionism and other toxicities.

Likewise, be selective in the media you consume. We all have our need for escapism, but, as much as possible, your "inputs" should delight and inspire you, not bore you or drag you down.

Speaking of community, empowered and authentic people seek happiness, health, and success not just for themselves, but others. That's partly because they want to pay it forward for help that they themselves received and/or privilege they benefited from, and partly because they know that you can't be truly happy or successful while those around you are suffering. And it's also because, on a deeper level, having your authentic needs met gives you the intellectual and emotional capacity to respond to others' needs with kindness, generosity, and care. Empowered and authentic people, in other words, do their best to see others not merely as competitors, or exploitable resources, or obstacles to their own (or society's) progress, but as the unique and valuable individuals they are—and, yes, that absolutely does include the precious nonhumans with whom we share the planet.

All of which brings us to my final piece of advice: *trust*.

Trust yourself: your skills, resources, capacities, and commitment. Trust that you are enough, and have enough, to succeed, especially if you use the techniques in this book to minimize your procrastination, perfectionism, unmanaged time, and other barriers. (As I've noted earlier, you may not actually have enough if you are being seriously disempowered by poverty, bigotry, and/or violence, but it's even more important, in such situations, to use the techniques I've discussed to reclaim whatever power you can.)

Trust that you can have a satisfying, fulfilling, and, at least sometimes, joyful life and career. They may not be exactly the life and career you are currently envisioning—possibly not even close. But any path built on empowerment and authenticity will have its substantial rewards. Trust the path.

Trust, also, your community. You are surrounded by visionary and powerful teachers, healers, creators, communicators, and seekers after equality and justice in all their forms. Find them, and live and work as much as possible among them.

Most of all, trust in the possibility of positive growth and change, both for individuals and societies, because—despite the easy, and often loud, pessimism of the doom-mongers—the evidence for that is all around us.

In fact, you're holding a bit of that evidence in your hands right now.

My own journey brought me to writing this book, and your own journey brought you to reading it. I am grateful that our paths crossed and wish you well, with all my heart, as you continue on yours.

Hillary Rettig
Kalamazoo, MI
November 2023

Acknowledgments

I gratefully acknowledge the assistance of:

Lee Busch, for yet another fantastic book cover.

Liz Alton, Alexis Diller, and Joan Frantschuk, for invaluable marketing and strategic advice.

Jan Tobochnik, for epic love and support, as well as terrific strategic advice.

My workshop students and coaching clients, for learning, insight, and inspiration.

If This Book Has Helped You...

If this book has helped you, please support my work by:
- Leaving a review on your favorite online bookseller. (Even a one- or two-line review is great!)
- Emailing any comments or suggestions for the next edition to me at hillary@hillaryrettig.com.
- Signing up for my mailing list at https://www.hillaryrettigproductivity.com. (You'll find many free articles and a couple of free downloadable ebooks there.)
- Inviting me to lead a workshop at your school, arts, community, parenting, or other group. (Email me at hillary@hillaryrettig.com with information about your group, and some possible dates.)

Thank you!

Hillary

About the Author

Along with the book you're holding, Hillary Rettig is also author of *Productivity is Power I: 5 Liberating Practices for College Students* (Infinite Art, 2022), *The Journey is the Reward: Fifteen Years of Blogging on Productivity, Life, and Love* (Infinite Art, 2023), *The 7 Secrets of the Prolific: The Definitive Guide to Overcoming Procrastination, Perfectionism, and Writer's Block* (Infinite Art, 2011), and *The Lifelong Activist: How to Change the World Without Losing Your Way* (Lantern Books, 2006).

She has taught productivity and time management classes at top educational, community, arts, and business organizations throughout the United States and beyond. Her articles have appeared in dozens of publications, including *Wired*, *Working Woman*, *Psychology Today*, *Fortune*, *Future Buzz*, *Time Management Ninja*, *Tomorrow's Professor*, *Authors Helping Authors*, and *The Thesis Whisperer*.

From 2001 – 2012, she worked as a microenterprise coach and microlender at two nonprofit agencies in Boston, roles in which she helped hundreds of people from all backgrounds start and grow businesses in fields including art, technology, personal services, professional services, manufacturing, distribution, and retail.

Hillary is also a vegan, a free software/free culture advocate, and a lover of life, dogs, and social justice in all its forms. She is also a living kidney donor and a former foster mother to four teenage South Sudanese refugees, now all adults and living independently.

Hillary was born in the Bronx, has spent time in Ithaca, New York, and Boston, Massachusetts, and now lives in Kalamazoo, Michigan, with her partner Jan Tobochnik, a physics professor at Kalamazoo College.

Visit https://www.hillaryrettigproductivity.com for free articles and downloads, and to sign up for Hillary's mailing list.

Other Books by Hillary Rettig

Productivity is Power I: 5 Liberating Practices for College Students

The 7 Secrets of the Prolific

The Lifelong Activist

The Journey is the Reward